SELF-EMPLOYMENT FOR DISABLED PEOPLE
EXPERIENCES FROM AFRICA AND ASIA

SELF-EMPLOYMENT FOR DISABLED PEOPLE

EXPERIENCES FROM AFRICA AND ASIA

Malcolm Harper and Willi Momm

International Labour Office   Geneva

ISBN 92-2-106457-3

First published 1989

Printed by the International Labour Office, Geneva, Switzerland

Acknowledgements

A book of this kind clearly owes a great deal more to the numerous people who provided the information on which it is based than to the authors whose names appear on the cover.

The greatest debt is of course owed to the 53 disabled entrepreneurs who so willingly gave up their time to talk to the investigators. They not only answered our questions, but also volunteered a great deal of additional information which was in many ways as valuable as the specific answers requested in our questionnaires; like all good respondents to surveys of this kind, they told us many of the questions we should have been asking. It was impossible to include detailed case studies of every one of them, but all their stories were inspiring, fascinating and humbling to those of us who have done so much less with so much more.

The staff of the 32 institutions who told us about their work also made an important contribution. The book contains many recommendations as to how disabled people can effectively be assisted to become self-employed, the majority of which were suggested by what the respondent institutions are already doing. One of the main purposes of this book is to share their experience with other institutions that wish to enter this field. The names of these institutions are listed at the end of the book.

We were fortunate to be able to benefit from the services of very talented and committed external collaborators, who carried out the field investigations in the six countries. They provided timely and comprehensive information, and made up for many of the weaknesses of the questionnaires by their sensitive approach and active collaboration. They were in fact co-authors rather than research assistants, and it is appropriate to list their names at this point: Mr. M.M. Jarboh and Mr. S. Mendy (Gambia); Mr. G.T. Matta and Mr. G.R. Srinivasan (India); Ms. Chodiraton (Indonesia); Mr. F.K. Boit (Kenya); Ms. C. Toledanotolosa (Philippines) ; Mr. T. Gudanga and Mr. D. Mudombi (Zimbabwe).

Finally, Adrian Nelson, Kate Harper and Derry Young provided valuable assistance with data analysis and typing.

Malcolm Harper is Professor at the Cranfield School of Management in the United Kingdom. Willi Momm is Senior Rehabilitation Officer in the Vocational Rehabilitation Branch of the ILO.

Contents

Introduction:
What is this book about?

This book is the outcome of an inquiry carried out in 1987 in the Gambia, India, Indonesia, Kenya, the Philippines and Zimbabwe. The purpose was to obtain information about disabled people who are in business on their own account and to show how they have managed.

The authors of this book – one a small enterprise development specialist and the other a rehabilitation professional – have come together for an unusual task: to see what disabled people can achieve as entrepreneurs and to examine the potential of self-employment as a viable prospect for disabled people who want to make a living.

Chapter 1 introduces the wider context and summarises the three main objectives that the authors set out to achieve; to call into question much of the conventional wisdom about disability; to provide encouragement to both disabled entrepreneurs and institutions serving them; and to suggest a fresh approach to rehabilitation. Chapter 2 then highlights the option of self-employment for disabled people seeking economic independence.

Chapter 3 – the core of the book – presents 16 case studies of disabled entrepreneurs chosen from the 53 businesses studied during the inquiry. The case studies are divided into three groups: those enterprises which are partially dependent on continuing assistance, those which once received assistance and those which have managed entirely on their own. A commentary is given on each group, the purpose being to demonstrate how disabled people succeed in self-employment and to obtain a better understanding of the nature of the problems they face when starting a business of their own.

These experiences are discussed in Chapter 4 in relation to normal small enterprise development. We identify the needs and problems common to disabled entrepreneurs and look into the various possibilities of enhancing the option of self-employment.

Chapter 5 examines what is being done for disabled entrepreneurs, drawing on the experience of 32 rehabilitation institutions in Africa and Asia that were included in the inquiry. It looks at how far the objectives of rehabilitation, the training offered, support services and follow-up are appropriate to the disabled clients and meet their needs.

The lessons to be learned from the analysis, both by disabled entrepreneurs and by rehabilitation institutions, are summarised in Chapter 6. Finally Chapter 7 offers some thoughts to planners concerned with establishing practical and appropriate services designed to promote self-help and self-reliance for disabled people.

1

The purpose of this book

Challenging myths and attitudes

The evidence from our inquiry challenges a number of myths traditionally associated with the image of disability. Equally important, however, it goes against false expectations that self-employment is the easy way out in the same way as it throws doubts on the placement records of many rehabilitation centres which conveniently classify their graduates as "self-employed" when placement in formal employment was no success. In short, this book sets objective facts against – and thus queries – deeply rooted attitudes among the general public, disabled people themselves and, last but not least, rehabilitation workers.

The general public will need to acknowledge the fact that not all disabled people are content to make a living through begging, or are happy to depend on social welfare or charity. Disabled people, like others, seek and obtain qualifications and use them to gain employment and income. This partly contradicts the general impression of disability which instinctively implies that some form of social welfare and protection is the answer and that disabled people are unsuitable for serious business. Nevertheless, it is dangerous to see only bias and prejudice in the view that disabled people need special protection. Many of them are incapable of coping with the tough realities of the world of work, or, too often, believe that they cannot do it.

There is understandable apprehension about the ability of the disabled to establish a viable business. "It is hard enough for them to find jobs: How can they possibly create them?" Reactions like this, however, do not only show lack of confidence in the abilities of disabled people, but reflect a typical view about self-employment: that it is one step beyond employment by others, and something more difficult which requires greater powers. The book investigates this issue.

The attitudes of the disabled themselves are more important than those of the general public when it comes to determining the viability of self-employment for disabled people. The concept of a business person – be it the most humble street vendor – is in definite contrast to the widespread image that many disabled people have of themselves: to have a right to be taken care of, to expect others to take decisions on their behalf and to wait for job offers rather than take the initiative in seeking employment. For the disabled reader, this book offers some hard evidence as to what is possible if one is prepared to take one's destiny into one's own hands.

Furthermore, the attitudes of the very people whose job it is to assist the disabled may be counter-productive to the promotion of self-employment. Many rehabilitation workers know little about the world for which they claim to prepare their disabled clients. Therefore considerable rethinking and readjustment are necessary before the rehabilitation system can respond to the challenge of preparing disabled people for self-employment. In fact, research shows that the successful businesses of many disabled people developed largely with the help of the family and the community and without much assistance from rehabilitation institutions.

The book gives evidence of a simple truth: to develop a business requires a good opportunity and the right state of mind, which means willingness to take risks, ability to work hard and above all an entrepreneurial spirit. The actual disability, by contrast, does not often seem to have been an impediment. Quite to the contrary, it is often the source of an extraordinary and inspiring effort.

These points are illustrated by the carefully selected case studies in this book, which show how people in various African and Asian countries have fared in establishing and running their businesses. There are examples of people who have managed without external assistance and who have struggled in extremely difficult economic conditions to generate income for themselves and their families. These cases are real and concrete and have given this book its special character: it reflects the experience of ordinary people in Africa and Asia rather than the theories or wishful thinking of development specialists. Even though these people may in the meantime have expanded their businesses or failed, their histories were found to be so rich in examples that the authors felt it legitimate to base their conclusions largely on them.

The evidence of the inquiry and the examples chosen make a case for self-employment as one possible option for disabled people. For those who assist disabled people but are not familiar with this approach, this book may serve as a guide and as a source of reference. It should lead to a better understanding of the reasons for the success or failure of self-employment endeavours.

Providing encouragement

To the careful reader the book will provide encouragement. Self-employment, properly tackled, is and remains a viable income-generating option for some disabled people. Certainly, more disabled people than are today involved in self-employment could become entrepreneurs. However, it is useless embarking upon a business unprepared and without having answered some hard questions for oneself. These questions apply to every future business person and usually have very little to do with the disability. For most potential disabled entrepreneurs, disability means reduced mobility. This may require certain conditions of housing or transport, and may predetermine the choice of products and services. Once the right choice has been made and arrangements made to facilitate it, the disability ceases to play a role. Therefore, disability is highlighted only for the purpose of this book. For the people interviewed it has lost its significance: they are first and foremost entrepreneurs and as such business problems have become more relevant to them than their physical or other handicaps.

The book should thus encourage potential entrepreneurs not to be overwhelmed by their disability or by the low social status that society usually accords to a disabled individual.

It is not an intention, however, to provide encouragement only to disabled individuals and those advising and assisting them, but also to those who control resources and who might not usually consider a disabled person to be worth the smallest amount of credit. Here the facts may speak for themselves and the book could become a powerful instrument for arguing the case of the disabled with those who control funds and expertise for self-employment ventures, whether small business advisory agencies, banks, government departments or technical assistance programmes promoting self-employment. The message is that disabled people should be judged on their merits and should have fair access to support and equal opportunities with their non-disabled peers.

The book, though focusing on developing countries, may also be of interest to disabled people in industrialised countries. With rampant unemployment among disabled people in these countries, the example of such people managing their own businesses successfully in far less advantageous conditions could stimulate new thinking among the disabled and a review of their options. In addition to the alternatives of a pension or a job on the open labour market, they might consider the possibility of self employment.

Changing rehabilitation approaches

Finally, the book deals with a subject which may have the potential for remoulding traditional rehabilitation approaches, at least in developing countries. It appears fairly accurate to say that the established system finds it difficult to perceive the disabled client as a future entrepreneur and consequently to awaken and promote entrepreneurial skills. Wherever disabled people develop such skills they do so outside rather than inside rehabilitation institutions. Institutions such as special schools for the blind, the deaf and mute and the physically handicapped, as well as many vocational rehabilitation centres and even production workshops for the disabled, show a tendency to overprotect the disabled and to instil in them the notion that they will eventually be taken care of. Because they are accustomed to turn to others for help, many disabled people end up as educated beggars in the streets once they leave institutions and face the struggle for survival. Begging is certainly the most common way of turning a physical disadvantage into an economic advantage, but rehabilitation services which produce beggars have failed to do their job.

Therefore this book may help rehabilitation workers and agencies to acquire a new outlook. Pity and overprotection are completely inadequate to prepare disabled people for self-employment – that is, for making a living through production, services or trading under one's own responsibility. The almost universal assumption that the disabled need charity or the support of social workers is to be questioned. There are indeed disabled people who need love, care, shelter, protection and constant support from others; however, there are also those who need assistance towards self-help, training to cope better with their handicap, an opportunity to develop their skills and short-term assistance to overcome their disadvantage and to give them a fair chance to compete on an equal level with non-disabled people. The self-employed disabled people who contributed to this book by telling us their life histories show us that there is a need for new approaches to rehabilitation; their stories contain a message with which rehabilitation practitioners have still to come to grips.

Whom is the book for?

The ideal readers of this book would be disabled people with the problem of how to support themselves. They would, we hope, be exposed to the possibilities of self-employment but also warned of the difficulties. We must accept, however, that it is unlikely that many copies of this book will fall into the hands of such people; many of them are in any case illiterate, at least in the languages in which it is likely to be available, and they lack access to the channels through which this book, or any similar publications, are likely to be distributed.

We must therefore move one stage back from the intended beneficiaries to those whose job it is to assist them. Basically, the book is addressed to two different groups of readers. First, and perhaps most obviously, it should introduce the idea of self-employment to staff of rehabilitation organisations and show them some of the pitfalls and opportunities. Second, we hope that at least some of the many official and non-governmental organisations that assist new and small enterprises in virtually every country will realise, as a result of reading this book, that disabled people represent an important source of potential entrepreneurs.

Both types of institution are already to a varying degree involved in assisting disabled people, and we do not wish to give the impression that those concerned with rehabilitation are totally unaware of the possibilities of self-employment or that agencies promoting new enterprises take no account of disabled people.

In fact, a number of specific initiatives are being introduced by such institutions: the Small Enterprise Development Organisation of Malawi, for instance, has set up a revolving loan fund especially for disabled borrowers, and the Lesotho Bank will likewise soon start a similar scheme. In India many local banks already have a policy of granting loans to disabled entrepreneurs.

There are, nevertheless, perhaps even larger numbers of staff in institutions of both types who are unaware of how some disabled people can gain enormously from self-employment. We hope that this book will stimulate them to become involved in this field and to extend their assistance to disabled people who might consider self-employment as an option, or are already self-employed.

2

Self-employment – an option for disabled people

Defining the terms

For the purposes of this book, we shall adopt broad and deliberately imprecise general guide-lines. By a disabled person we mean anyone who experiences significant limitations in one or several functions because of a physical, sensorial or mental impairment or deficiency. On account of these limitations, and of the negative societal attitudes which often go with it, the person who has a handicap will most likely experience restrictions in the ability fully to develop his or her potential and to earn a living. Disability may or may not affect the ability to work, but a disabled person will usually have to cope with many more problems than would a non-disabled person. However, it is a misconception – suggested by the term disability and nourished by common prejudice – that disability means inability to work.

The decision as to whether a particular person does or not fall into the category of "disabled people" is clearly affected not only by physical condition, but also by living conditions and the availability of artificial aids. A strong pair of spectacles, an artificial limb or even a wheelchair might move someone out of our definition, and a person living in a remote rural area with no roads which can be used by wheeled vehicles may be more "disabled" than someone with the same or greater physical disability who lives in a town and is well served by public transport. The disabled people referred to in this book are therefore ordinary people who are fit for work, ready to become entrepreneurs and able to earn a living for themselves and their families. The special handicap with which they must cope could be their private affair. However, as a disability often goes hand in hand with discrimination and the denial of equal opportunities in education, training and employment, disabled people do require positive and supportive interventions on their behalf.

"Self-employment", "small enterprise" and such terms are similarly fraught with definitional problems. Here again, we shall select a meaning which is appropriate for our purpose regardless of any lack of precision or alternative views. Our concern in this book, as reflected in the case studies, lies mainly with the very smallest type of enterprise that employs few workers, maybe only the owner.

Larger enterprises are outside the scope of this book because once an enterprise has reached the stage of employing a significant number of employees, it is unlikely to need the same kind of support as one which is just being started, whether or not its owner is disabled; and this book is intended principally for those concerned with identifying ways in which disabled people can become self-sufficient, rather than with helping those who have already achieved this.

It is important to distinguish self-employment from subsidised and protected employment such as sheltered workshops or income-generating schemes funded by assistance agencies. Many severely disabled people may always need a degree of employment assistance, whether in the form of voluntary or otherwise subsidised management, an especially protected market, supplies of raw materials, provision of workshops or other forms of shelter from the pressures of the competitive world of business. The exclusion of a "business" of this kind, except as a route to what we call genuine self-employment, should not be interpreted to mean that it is not an appropriate solution. For some people, a sheltered environment will remain the only way of partaking in productive activities and of experiencing a certain degree of economic independence and recognition. However, such an enterprise can be considered as self-employment within the terms of reference of this book only if the employees themselves take over and manage it on a self-sustaining basis.

Self-employment is not for everyone

It is important to stress from the outset that self-employment is not a panacea through which every disabled person, or even a large proportion of the disabled, can become self-supporting and thus avoid the need for further assistance. "Entrepreneurship" is a dangerously fashionable term, and many governments and others are grasping at the concept of "enterprise" as the solution to all their economic problems. Only a minority of any given population is likely to possess the necessary attributes to start their own enterprise successfully. Even in the so-called "informal sector" in urban areas of many developing countries, where nearly everyone appears to be self-employed, it is clear on closer observation that most of them are actually employees working for smaller numbers who make the decisions as to what is bought, made and sold, and at what price.

The position of disabled people is no different; although some may be forced into self-employment because their disability disqualifies them from other forms of livelihood, there are many others whose disability makes them less likely to be able to start their own enterprises. Their physical incapacity may be such as to make self-employment impossible or very difficult, or the reactions of their families or the community to their disability may have the effect of reducing their self-confidence and making them less rather than more able to take the initiative.

It is, of course, impossible to state what proportion of any population of disabled people may reasonably be considered as potential entrepreneurs and expected to do the kind of things that the people described later in this book have been able to do. As pointed out above, the restrictions imposed by a disability may or may not affect the person's ability to work. This depends very much on individual circumstances, and for that reason no general conclusions can be drawn with respect to the appropriateness of certain types of jobs for people with certain types of disabilities. Quite contrary to common prejudice, which tends to associate certain disabilities with certain jobs, it is an established principle that each case requires individual assessment. This clearly means that the feasibility of a self-employment venture can be determined only when taking into account the very special circumstances of the individual. Not only does the disability count but even more the environment (e.g. family support, community attitudes, mobility problems or the market). But successful self-employment will above all else depend on whether the person has the necessary combination of personal characteristics to make him or her an entrepreneur. Although it is possible, as will be discussed later, to create or at least to reveal and enhance the personal characteristics which contribute to entrepreneurial success, it is neither humane, feasible nor cost effective to try to persuade or encourage any but a small minority of the disabled – or of any other group of people – to take this step.

Why self-employment?

There are a number of different ways in which people can attain economic independence. Self-employment is only one of them and must be compared with alternatives by disabled people themselves and by anyone who is trying to assist them to support themselves fully or in part. It would be altogether wrong if this book were to encourage institutions and policy-makers to promote self-employment as a universal solution, or even as a limited one, if the disabled people or the environment are not appropriate.

The unemployed person seeking employment in private business or government is fundamentally dependent on somebody else deciding to employ him or her. Self-employment is basically different; the unemployed person decides to start an enterprise, however small, and although its success depends on other people being willing to buy from and sell to it, for whatever motives, the decision to start it depends on the individual concerned.

Jobs on the open labour market become more and more scarce. Self-employment may therefore be the only practicable option for many people; however, there are many other reasons why this option, and the myriad of small enterprises that result from people choosing it, are a good thing for national development. This applies whether the entrepreneur is disabled or not; there are certain reasons, which we shall shortly examine, why this option is particularly suitable for disabled people, and others why it is particularly difficult.

In economic terms, self-employment represents possibly the most cost-effective way of creating jobs. The capital requirements are usually very small; perhaps the commonest form of new enterprise is the market vendor whose "fixed capital" may amount to no more than a basket or a sheet of plastic on which to display whatever is sold and whose "working capital" probably consists of sales worth no more than a day, half a day or even an hour. Such enterprises often "squat" on the verandas of existing businesses, or on roadsides or open ground without using any costly infrastructure.

New manufacturing, trading or service enterprises use a minimum of capital and a maximum amount of labour because the objective of the entrepreneur is often to buy a job; necessarily, he or she will keep the cost of the job in terms of capital requirements as low as possible. Since one of the common features of developing countries is their shortage of capital and surplus of labour, any form of employment creation which makes minimum use of the former and maximum use of the latter is clearly to be preferred.

There are other arguments in favour of new small enterprises as a form of economic growth and employment creation. Transport facilities for people and for merchandise in most developing countries are often overloaded and unreliable, and they use scarce foreign resources in terms of vehicles and fuel. A person wanting to start a business will be likely to do it near to or actually in his or her own home. Working for other people, unless it is within a family enterprise, almost inevitably involves travelling, often for long distances from peripheral squatter locations to central industrial areas or business districts.

These enterprises also tend to use readily available materials and to sell to local people; this means that they make still lower demands on transport facilities than enterprises which draw their employees and materials from long distances and which sell to customers in other parts of the country or even abroad.

Small businesses usually start where people live and continue to be local. They also provide goods and services which are economical, in terms both of cost and of the places and times where they are available. They are therefore appropriate in that they produce goods that poor people need at prices they can afford and when and where they need them. Planners, and the wealthy minority whose cars are delayed in streets crowded with vendors and small repair shops and manufacturers, may be irritated by these small enterprises, but the majority benefit by selling to them, buying from them and working in them.

Such enterprises do not usually earn foreign exchange by exporting, although handicrafts are often bought by foreign tourists; they do, however, save foreign exchange by making the maximum use of local equipment and materials. More importantly perhaps, they rarely, if ever, make any demands on foreign expertise and finance. Even when the entrepreneur is able to take advantage of special assistance schemes, the amount of capital used for each job created is almost always less than for larger enterprises. Such businesses are also necessarily appropriate in terms of the skills they demand of their owners. Vendors and roadside mechanics may not manage their enterprises with business school skills or employ the latest high technology methods, but they do make the optimum use of local labour as well as physical resources.

Finally, enterprises which are started by local people, particularly in rural areas, tend to be enterprises involving the whole family. The mutual support and security that this system provides makes it particularly suitable for disadvantaged groups.

The position of the disabled

The reader may already have picked out from this general survey of the advantages of new small enterprises those aspects which are particularly relevant to the disabled in a positive or negative sense. It is fairly clear that disabled people are more likely to be poor than others from the same socio-economic level, if only because they have had few opportunities to save money from previous earnings. Since disabled people often have no capital at all, the choice for them is not between starting a large capital-intensive enterprise or a small one, but between starting a small enterprise, trying to find a job or continuing to be totally dependent on family, charity or public assistance.

In respect of capital, therefore, the disabled are at a grave disadvantage; this partly explains why those enterprises which they do engage in tend to be those which require the very lowest amounts of capital, as for example petty vending or personal services such as massage or shoe-shining.

Disabled people are also less likely than others to have received an adequate formal education. There is very little evidence that higher education, or even advanced secondary education, is necessary or desirable for successful entrepreneurs, but basic literacy and numeracy are useful, if not essential, as countries develop and the communications infrastructure becomes more widespread. Those without these basic skills become more and more disadvantaged.

In addition, many disabled people are used to a sheltered and protected environment where they have little or no opportunity to make decisions and are expected to acquiesce quietly and cause a minimum of trouble. Excessive humility is a poor basis for enterprise; if people expect a disabled person to be helpless, it is all too easy for him or her to satisfy their expectations.

Most obviously, of course, disability means what it says. People who suffer from the loss or impairment of one function, whether it be sight or hearing, or who cannot use their hands or legs as effectively as others, are disadvantaged. Other facilities may become exceptionally well developed as a form of compensation but disability frequently means less ability to do the very job one is best suited for. Since self-employment requires ability of a high level, a disabled person may be less competitive in his performance than a non-disabled person.

There are some reasons, however, why self-employment may be more attractive to disabled people than to others who may in any case be able to find work in existing enterprises. Finding a job usually means going out and looking for it, queueing at a labour exchange, rushing quickly to building sites at the rumour of work or travelling extensively within the country or even abroad. Disability almost always implies some loss of mobility; it is easier, if potentially less remunerative, for a disabled person to start some form of enterprise at home or very close to home than to travel in search of work.

Family support is also even more important for the disabled than for others without work. Although some forms of disability, such as leprosy, may lead to ostracism by the community and even the family, it is usual for a family to accept responsibility for disabled members, as they do for other family members who cannot support themselves. If disabled people have to leave home to find work, they will not only find it difficult to travel but will also be deprived of the family's support. Those who can work at or near their homes can move gradually from total dependence towards independence, as far as is feasible, while still enjoying a certain degree of support from their families.

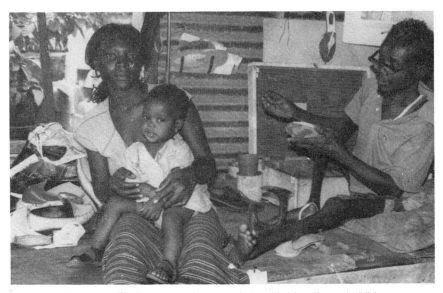

Mohamed Kagbo, a Zimbabwean shoe repairer, with his wife and child

Discouragement from self-employment

Success in self-employment, as in any other endeavour, is more a function of psychological factors and motivation than it is of physical resources. Everyone can think of numerous examples of people who have enjoyed massive support and every possible advantage and have failed, while there are others who have had to overcome overwhelming disadvantages and have enjoyed no external support but have nevertheless succeeded. We should therefore examine the possible effects of disability on the motivation of the disabled in order to identify those characteristics which may or may not be conducive to self-employment.

In many, if not most, societies, people who are disabled are regarded as just that. Even if their disability relates only to one faculty, such as sight, hearing or use of the arms or legs, there is a tendency for others to believe that they cannot do anything at all, or at least as well as those who are not disadvantaged in the same way.

Most human accomplishments require a subtle combination of faculties. A pianist must read the music, hear what he or she plays, use both hands on the keyboard and both feet on the pedals, and must also be able to sit upright in order to play. People are amazed when a blind person becomes a talented or even a virtuoso pianist, as many have. Sighted people cannot understand how the pianist has developed his or her other faculties in order to overcome the lack of sight since they do not have to do it themselves, and there is a tendency to admire what we cannot understand.

This admiration is a function of our expectation that disabled people will not be able to perform as well as others. It is well known that people who are not trusted tend over time actually to become untrustworthy, and that children whom their teachers expect to perform well do in fact perform well because of the teachers' expectations. In the same way, if a person is expected by those around him, including his family, fellow students and most people with whom he is in daily contact, to be less capable than others, he will in due course actually behave as expected.

The decision to become self-employed is as much as anything else a function of self-confidence, and the same may be said of success in self-employment. If a person's confidence has been continually eroded by the expectations of those around him or her, the effect on actual performance will be more serious than for a potential entrepreneur who has a support network of colleagues and superiors.

Reference has already been made to the ways in which leprosy patients are ostracised in that people are unwilling to have any physical contact with them or even to touch anything they have touched. This is clearly an extreme case – although such behaviour is not based on medical evidence – but disability is often regarded as a curse so that contact with disabled people is avoided at all costs. People who have been disabled since childhood are often hidden away by their families as objects of shame or because they may damage the marriage prospects of other family members; they may therefore come to perceive themselves as a burden to their families and of no value to society.

Ostracism, or even a milder version of deprivation of social contact, is even more disadvantageous to someone who is self-employed than to someone who is employed by others. An employee can work in isolation as a carpenter, a computer programmer or on an assembly line, more or less independently of contact with others, but someone who is self-employed must have regular and sustained contact with suppliers and, most importantly, with customers.

New small enterprises usually operate in highly competitive markets. If there are ten or more vegetable vendors selling similar produce at similar prices, many customers may avoid buying from the one whom they have been conditioned to avoid since childhood. This is particularly likely to be the case when the disabled business person actually comes from the community where he or she is working. We have already seen that the relative immobility of the disabled makes self-employment at home particularly attractive, but doing business in your own community may mean having to sell to people who have hitherto avoided you and tended to deny that you existed. This "social disability" also extends to finance, purchasing, licences, permission to operate and all the other resources which a self-employed person needs and which require personal contact and perseverance.

Motivation for self-employment

This form of ostracism or exclusion from society may, however, be more than outweighed by the sympathy which many people feel for the disabled. Some may avoid them but others may give them preference when making buying decisions, allocating space or giving licences in the same way that some firms give special preference to disabled employees. Many disabled people, and particularly those who are of the type to want to become self-employed, might be reluctant to accept this element of charity or support, but it has to be accepted like any other fact and it may in some cases make all the difference between failure and success.

There are a number of other positive factors which may make it easier rather than harder for some disabled people to survive in their own businesses. Entrepreneurship is frequently associated with the will to overcome the state of "social marginality"; people who are in some way excluded from society often derive from this the motivation to take the risky and original initiative of starting their own enterprise. This may be because they have no alternative.

One case in point may be refugees, who are perhaps the most obviously marginalised group. They usually arrive in their host country with little more than the clothes they stand up in, having often suffered physically and psychologically during their flight from their own country. Yet in spite of these difficulties, or perhaps because of them, refugees have, through self-employment, become prosperous members of their new countries and have often made a major contribution to their economic development.

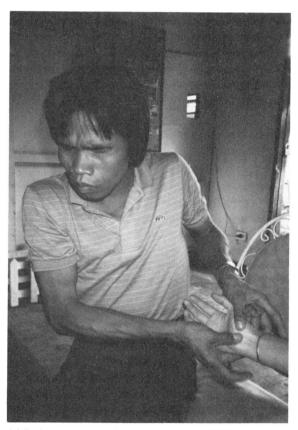

A blind masseur working in the Philippines

It is often the psychological condition of disabled people that makes them particularly likely to do well and persevere in self-employment, for if this is successful, it is also a particularly effective way of establishing somebody's confidence and of achieving genuine rehabilitation not only of the body but also of the spirit.

Disability can also be a stimulus for independent problem-solving and innovation. Disabled children often develop new and effective ways of moving around, communicating or otherwise overcoming their problems. Nobody in the family or the community has been faced with the same problem before. The experience of facing and coping with difficulties which are unfamiliar can be a valuable, if onerous, form of personal development. Entrepreneurs have been defined as "people who put things together in new ways". This is exactly what disabled people have to do.

In a more direct, physical sense, people who have lost the use of one faculty, or have never possessed it, are more likely to be able to concentrate single-mindedly on a task which needs the faculties that they do possess than those who possess other faculties which are not being used and are thus likely to be a source of distraction. Massage is perhaps the most obvious example; blind masseurs are well known for their skill, and there are many examples of blind people who are able to succeed partly because they can transmit all their skill and concentration through their fingers rather than being disturbed by sight, which is fundamentally unnecessary for massage.

Deaf people develop their own ways of keeping company with themselves without the distraction of conversation; if their business is of a kind where they do not regularly have to speak to other people or where such contact can be facilitated as necessary by outsiders, they may be particularly effective because of their ability to concentrate and to avoid distractions.

Working together

Self-employment has so far been treated exclusively as an individual activity undertaken by one person. It is important to stress that there are many examples of successful co-operatives or group enterprises where numbers of people have come together in order to pool their resources and their skills and to start a business together. This form of self-employment has many advantages; people can share the numerous responsibilities of business, they can take advantage of the economies in purchasing and operations that arise from the larger scale of their enterprise, and they can benefit from the mutual support and encouragement of their fellow members rather than having to labour alone.

The record of group enterprise, however, is far less successful than that of individual business, in spite of the obvious advantages. The commonest reason for the failure of such enterprises is the failure of the group to work together effectively; jealousies arise, members do not accept leadership from among themselves, and the end result is most frequently one of two disappointments: either the group breaks up and the enterprise ceases to operate or the group is "hijacked" by a particular individual who often exploits his or her fellow members and runs the enterprise for selfish ends.

Disabled people, like other marginalised groups, are particularly likely to be able to work together effectively because they share a common problem and feel that they must stick together in order to show the rest of the world that they can succeed. Groups or co-operatives of disabled people, like any other enterprise, must be effectively led; they must avoid being used by political interests and they must be managed in a businesslike way using the necessary skills to produce goods or services at a price that others are willing to pay. Such groups must also be genuinely "owned" and managed by their members, rather than being dependent on outside financing and direction. It is vitally important for anyone who is assisting disabled people to work together with them to ensure that the initiative and control belong to the group rather than coming from outside. If this can be achieved, disabled people may be more likely than most to overcome the problems of group enterprise and to exploit the undoubted advantages.

3

Disabled entrepreneurs:
Case studies

The sample

We have examined the arguments for self-employment and have identified reasons why this option may or may not be an appropriate one for disabled people as a way of supporting themselves. We shall now look at a number of individual enterprises, owned and run by disabled people; this will illustrate how their founders and owners have overcome the difficulties which face anyone, particularly a disabled person, who wishes to become self-employed, and will also show how others have failed because they could not overcome these problems.

It is important to recognise that these examples or case studies are in no way representative of all enterprises run by disabled people; so small a number could never hope to illustrate more than a few aspects of the problems and opportunities involved in self-employment.

The case studies have been selected from a survey of 53 small enterprises owned and managed by disabled people. The survey was undertaken in Gambia, India, Indonesia, Kenya, the Philippines and Zimbabwe. The actual enterprises covered in each country were chosen in order to be approximately representative of the disabled people with whom each of the individual interviewers was in contact. Since these interviewers work for rehabilitation organisations, they clearly had a tendency to contact people who had been assisted by their own or similar institutions. They were asked to include a number of enterprises which had never received any official assistance from any source, but enterprises of this type are inevitably underrepresented since the interviewers naturally found it easier to contact those whom they already knew.

Before turning to the case studies, we briefly summarise the most important features of the group of 53 enterprises which were surveyed; again, it is important to stress that the whole group, like the smaller number described in the case studies, is not a representative sample of small enterprises owned by disabled people. It would be wrong and dangerous to suggest that because particular types of businesses in the sample had succeeded more than others, or because people with a particular disability tended to be engaged in a particular type of enterprise, this is the most appropriate type of business for other disabled people to undertake. The data are given merely in order to illustrate the nature of the group of enterprises from which the case studies were selected; readers must judge the degree to which this group is similar to those with whom they themselves have to deal.

Countries:	Philippines	11
	Indonesia	4
	India	7
	Kenya	9
	Zimbabwe	6
	Gambia	6
Sex of owner:	Male	44
	Female	9
Type of business:	Shopkeepers and vendors	11
	Tailors	11
	Handicraft workers	9
	Cobblers	7
	Masseurs	2
	Others	13

The "others" included carpenters, training schools, radio repairers, transporters and toy-makers.

Type of organisation:	Sole proprietors	43
	Formal co-operatives	5
	Informal groups	4
	Societies	1
Period in business:	6 years or more	24
	3 to 5 years	18
	2 years or less	11

Complete loss of mobility through loss of leg functions (e.g. double amputation, paralysis, deformity)	16
Reduced mobility through restricted leg function (e.g. amputation of one leg, deformity in one or both legs, but moving possible with crutches, sticks, etc.)	16
Loss of sight or severe visual restriction	7
Loss of arm or hand functions with partial restriction in manual operations (e.g. amputation, leprosy or polio-induced deformity)	2
Loss of hearing and/or speaking ability	1
Others (including combination of above disabilities)	11

With regard to the underrepresentation of disabled women in the sample, it is important to point out that other surveys on self-employment report an equally low proportion of female entrepreneurs. This is not the place to look into the specific reasons for this pattern, but it is relevant to note that it concerns women in general and not disabled women alone. Even though it may be attributed to the traditional role of women in most of the developing countries, there is no reason to assume that women are in any way less able to be successfully self-employed. It has been estimated that there is no male earner in about one-third of all households in developing countries and that most of the female breadwinners depend on self-employment for their income. Evidence from many countries also shows that women are more likely to repay loans, and to make successful entrepreneurs, than men.

Traders and vendors are also somewhat underrepresented since in most countries small-scale entrepreneurs who sell things rather than make them usually total half or more of the self-employed. This feature of our sample may be due to the fact that only a quarter of the disabled people had not had any external assistance in starting their enterprises. Petty trading is the most obvious form of self-employment, particularly for the disabled, since it requires no specialised skills and a minimum of initial capital. It is probable that if the sample had been more representative and had been made up mainly of those who had never received any official assistance, more of them would have been vendors and shopkeepers.

The survey also covered 32 rehabilitation institutions for disabled people, at least some of whose ex-trainees go on to become self-employed. We shall discuss the results of this part of the survey in Chapter 5, but it may be appropriate at this stage to mention the enormous range of different types of enterprise which were mentioned by the various institutions.

It might be thought that disabled people, if they can start any kind of business, would be restricted to traditional and familiar activities such as tailoring, joinery and handicrafts. The following case studies show that this is by no means true and that disabled people can start and sustain just as varied a range of enterprises as anyone else. The list of enterprises run by ex-trainees of the 32 institutions runs to approximately 100 different trades; as might have been expected, tailoring was the most popular, followed by carpentry, basket weaving, leather work and shopkeeping, but there were also a large number of far less familiar types of business, many of which were mentioned by several of the institutions, and of which there are many hundreds owned and managed by disabled people.

The following sample gives some idea of the variety included in the list:

Sign writing	Farming
Lottery ticket sales	Poultry-keeping
Milk selling	Transport services
Bookbinding	Screen printing
Welding	Picture-framing
Umbrella repair	Phone booth operation
Taxi-driving	Goldsmith
Brick-making	Scrap metal dealing
Confectionery making	Toy shop
Shoe-cleaning	Cardboard folder making
Figurine moulding	Soap-making
Petrol selling	Library operation
Massage	Brassware-making
Water carts	Postage stamp selling
Photocopying	Licence acquisition
Railway ticket buying	Hotel
Pottery	Plant nursery
Appliance repair	

The list is remarkable not only for its diversity, but also for the fact that many of the activities, such as water selling or scrap metal dealing are often perceived as somehow illegitimate and representative of the "informal sector", which is regarded by uninformed observers to be an indicator of poverty rather than a means of survival. The fact that assistance institutions mention such activities shows that their staff at any rate are aware of the vital and continuing importance of informal enterprise, particularly for those who are most in need, and are proud of the fact that they have helped people to become employed in it.

Businesses such as operating 'phone booths or obtaining railway tickets and licences for a fee are also excellent examples of ways in which people who have restricted physical ability but are persistent, patient and efficient can make a living.

A trainee from the Fellowship of the Physically Handicapped operating a public telephone business in Bombay

We also collected information about the types of assistance, if any, that the business people had received or were presently receiving and about their customers, scale of business, problems and future plans. We shall present this information later in the course of our discussion of ways in which such people can most effectively be assisted. But we shall first examine 16 case studies in more detail.

It was difficult to decide in what sequence or categories the case studies should be presented in order to put over a coherent message. One could analyse them in terms of types or scale of business, the sex or age of the owners, or the countries where they operate. However, since the overall goal of the disabled people themselves and of those trying to help them is presumably self-sufficiency with no further assistance, the case studies have been chosen to illustrate varying degrees of dependence. We start with some examples of enterprises which are still receiving outside help of various kinds and to varying extents. We then go on to case studies which describe people who were at one time assisted with training, finance or in other ways and have now progressed to the level where they no longer need such help. Finally, we present descriptions of a number of disabled people who are in business for themselves and who have never enjoyed help from institutions as opposed to family sources.

The reader should not assume that assistance is unnecessary because the latter group comes last and might therefore be considered to be the ultimate or "best" form of disabled entrepreneurship. It is important to recognise, however, that the vast majority of disabled people who are self-employed have never received any official assistance at all. They have reached whatever level of success and self-sufficiency that they have achieved through their own efforts and with family support. Those who are trying to help other disabled people to do the same must be humble; they must face the fact that their efforts are unlikely ever to reach more than a small fraction of those who might be able to benefit from them. This does not mean that the assistance is unnecessary or trivial, but it is inevitably limited and exemplary. Its objective must be to help people who could not otherwise become self-employed to do so and to encourage others to do the same through the example of those who are successful. Excessive assistance, in fact, can be more dangerous than no assistance at all; it perpetuates dependence and creates the impression that disabled people cannot achieve self-sufficiency without massive help. The last set of case studies in this collection should effectively destroy this illusion.

Group I: Enterprises still receiving assistance

Mary Gwande: The Jerusalem Tailors' Co-operative

Mary Gwande, or Sister Mary Gwande as she is now called, is in her late 40s. When she was 3 years old she was injured in a fire; both her legs were amputated below the knee and she was confined to a wheelchair. Because of her disability, Mary was unable to go to school as a child, but she learned how to read and write on her own. This achievement was to serve her in good stead later in life.

In 1968, both Mary Gwande's parents died and she moved in with her brother. In the following year, she became a member of the Apostolic Faith, a rapidly growing Christian group in her area of Zimbabwe. Mary became a leading member of this church; the other members bought her a wheelchair and they later provided her with a place to stay.

In 1977 her brother, who works as a tailor for one of the country's leading clothing manufacturing companies, bought his sister a sewing-machine and some materials which were worth a total of 480 Zimbabwe dollars (US$1 = Z$1.65).[1] He then undertook to train his sister to use them, and she succeeded within only two months in becoming a competent tailor and also in learning the simple mathematics which were necessary to calculate the cost of what she was making. Armed with this knowledge, and with the machine, Mary then became an independent tailor.

Mary struggled on her own until 1984; there was a ready market for her garments, but because of her immobility she was unable to market her wares effectively. She had to wait for customers to come to her rather than going out to them and was therefore unable to keep herself fully occupied. Mary did try to find a donor to assist her to employ somebody who would sell on her behalf, but she was unsuccessful.

In 1984, therefore, Mary realised that she could no longer carry on as she had been doing; she approached her fellow members of the Apostolic Faith and suggested to them that they should form a co-operative enterprise. Thanks to Sister Gwande's efforts and the advice of the local community development worker, the Jerusalem Co-operative was formed in 1985 and started to operate in November of the same year. Sister Gwande was elected to head the co-operative and each of the members paid Z$25 as their initial contribution. They also had 12 sewing-machines between them, including that belonging to Sister Gwande, and they lent these to the co-operative.

In addition to Sister Gwande, three other members are also disabled; because of this, and also because the church wished to support this initiative of its members, the Apostolic Faith provided the women with a place where they could work free of charge. The Ministry of Community Development and Women's Affairs also gave them a grant of Z$814 which they used to buy materials together with the money they had invested themselves.

The Ministry helped the Jerusalem Co-operative to reach a loose agreement with two local schools to supply them with uniforms. After they had bought the materials, one of the schools changed the style of its uniforms, which meant that those which the Jerusalem Co-operative had made could not be sold to the school; they are in fact still trying to sell them elsewhere. The co-operative made a profit of Z$2,050 on the work for the other school; they shared approximately half this amount among themselves and put the balance in the bank.

The Jerusalem Co-operative is still operating, albeit on a reduced level, and the members are reluctant to spend more than two or three days a week working on it because they are not sure that it will be successful. This reluctance actually limits their success because they are unable to make clothes for sale to the general public and they would undoubtedly do better if they were to devote some time to obtaining orders from sources other than the schools which they are already supplying.

At the present time, the co-operative is receiving regular visits from the Ministry's social worker, together with substantial management assistance for which no charge is made. It is also continuing to occupy the free premises provided by the Apostolic Faith, and Sister Gwande is doing her best to encourage the members to devote more time and enthusiasm to their work.

The majority of the members who are not disabled spend most of their time working on their small farms and ekeing out a modest subsistence income in this way. Sister Gwande recognises that if they were to devote more time to the affairs of the co-operative, it would probably succeed, but most of the members are unwilling to do this unless somebody can prove to them beforehand that it will succeeed. This is obviously impossible, and Mary Gwande is still trying to find a way out of this difficult position.

The Oyugis Sheltered Workshop

In August 1986 a group of 25 people who were physically disabled in various different ways came together in an effort to earn a living for themselves instead of remaining perpetually dependent on their families. They had all received training in carpentry at a number of different youth centres and rehabilitation centres around Kenya. Some had been trained for 18 months, while others had received a full two-year training. The programmes at the training centres also included a certain amount of very basic management training since it is recognised in Kenya that a number of disabled people may start their own businesses, either because they find this an attractive option or because they have no alternative.

The members of the group were encouraged to come together by the availability of financing from the National Trust Fund for Disabled Persons, and they were fortunate enough to secure a substantial grant which paid for certain essential items of equipment that the members themselves had not yet been able to obtain.

The members informally constituted themselves into an informal self-help group and, with the assistance of the National Trust Fund for Disabled Persons, an administrator was appointed to organise and assist them in their endeavour.

The group manufactures high-quality furniture which is sold direct to members of the general public; overall responsibility for its affairs is in the hands of a committee which has been elected by the members, but actual day-to-day responsibility for managing the finance, production and personnel of the enterprise is in the hands of the administrator.

The group earns enough from its sales to pay an annual rent of 540 Kenya Shillings (US$1 = KSh16.71), to buy materials when these are not provided in advance by customers and to pay wages at a rather low and erratic rate. The administrator is paid by the National Trust Fund for Disabled Persons and the group also receives regular visits from a social worker who advises the administrator and the members on the particular problems that arise because of the members' physical disabilities.

The administrator does not keep any record of the annual sales of the Oyugis Workshop, nor is he aware of whether it makes any profit or not. He believes that the main problem is the shortage of cash, and if the group were able to accumulate some funds, he says, it could employ supervisors and build more workshops so that more disabled people could be accommodated. There does not, at the moment, appear to be any immediate chance of these goals being achieved.

Jambo's Shoe Repair business

Luwo Jambo was born approximately 50 years ago in Mozambique. When he was about 3 years old he fell into a fire and, as a result of the injuries he received, his right foot had to be amputated. Jambo remained in Mozambique until he was about 18 years old and never went to school. He had no access to any specialised facilities for his disability and moved around as well as he could on the stump of his amputated foot.

When he was 18, Jambo decided to migrate to Zimbabwe where he had contacts and where he believed it might be possible to make a better living. He had to bind a small piece of rubber tyre around the stump of his right foot in order to complete the long journey to Zimbabwe, but his efforts were rewarded. A year after he reached Harare, or Salisbury as it was then called, he obtained a job as a gardener and worked in this position for nine years. In 1964 his employer promoted him to the position of cook and he remained with the same family for a further 11 years until 1975.

During this period Jambo was able to attend night school and studied up to grade 5. His employer was not willing to buy him the special orthopaedic shoe which he needed to protect the stump of his right foot, but this disappointment was actually a blessing in disguise. Jambo approached a friend who was also from Mozambique and was employed as a shoemaker. This friend made Jambo an orthopaedic shoe and charged him a reasonable price for it. Jambo was so pleased that he decided to avoid being dependent on somebody else's generosity again; he asked his friend to teach him how to make a similar shoe for himself the next time.

As a result of this initial request, Jambo's friend took him on as an apprentice and in two years he learned enough, working on his days off and during the evenings, to be able to make orthopaedic shoes for himself. At the same time, of course, he learned how to make ordinary shoes and thus equipped himself to make a living on his own.

During this period, Jambo had married and had six children. He was therefore naturally anxious to increase his earnings, and in 1975, equipped with his new skill as a shoemaker, he moved out of Harare to an area called Domboshava, some 40 kilometres to the north.

Jambo opened his business at Nyakudua business centre in Domboshava, where he rented space on a veranda for Z$20 per month. He required hardly any initial capital since he had already bought himself a few simple tools during his period of apprenticeship and the initial supplies of materials cost only a negligible amount.

For two years Jambo continued working as a cobbler at Nyakudua but he never succeeded in getting enough business to make more than a marginal contribution to his earnings. He was, on occasion, unable even to pay his rent and in 1977 he left Nyakudua and moved to a neighbouring business centre called Masukandoro, partly because he was able to operate rent free there.

In the event, he was not more successful in Masukandoro; for two-and-a-half years he worked full time but then reduced this to only two days a week when he realised that there was no more demand than there had been in Nyakudua. During this period his sales were approximately Z$40 a month, and after paying for materials, this left him with approximately Z$30 per month. This was quite insufficient for him to maintain his family and he eventually gave up the shoemaking business altogether and concentrated in helping his family cultivate their small plot of land.

Jambo is naturally disappointed at the failure of his shoemaking business. When he left his job as a cook in Harare he had hoped substantially to increase his income and to be able to offer his family a better lifestyle. He believes that there are two major reasons for the failure of his enterprise. First, most people in Domboshava earn their living by growing vegetables which they take every day to sell in Harare. While they are in the capital city, they are able to take advantage of the enormous range of services available there, including great numbers of shoemakers. There is really no reason for them to purchase services of this kind locally since they go to Harare nearly every day in any case.

Second, Jambo believes that he failed because he was never able to accumulate enough capital to purchase the right tools and raw materials with which to offer a service which was competitive with that of other, more modern shoemakers. He had to use pieces of old rubber tyre, similar to that which he tied around his leg so many years before when he walked from Mozambique, instead of the specially moulded soles which customers now expect. His tools were also inadequate because he was never able to afford anything better and the standard of his work was such that it might be acceptable in the more remote areas but not in an area close to the capital city.

Jambo is not discouraged, however, and is still hoping that he will be able to obtain funds from some source or other in order to buy modern tools and good quality materials. He is in regular contact with a welfare assistance agency and plans to attend a two-month refresher course in shoemaking. He is also approaching various people whom he thinks will be able to help him buy better tools and materials.

Jambo hopes that he will be able in the future not only to earn his own living but also to train other disabled people as shoemakers. His dream is to found a co-operative through which a number of shoemakers, trained by him, would be able to buy materials in bulk and thus lower their cost of operations. They would run their businesses in different villages independently from one another but would, through their co-operative, be able to share experiences as well as bulk buying of raw materials, and would thus be able to produce other leather products when the demand for shoe repair was low.

Momodou Njie: The miller

Momodou Njie was born around 1940 in Kaur, a small town some 170 kilometres up the river Gambia from Banjul. When he was about 10 years old he contracted an eye disease and, as a result, lost the sight of his right eye. This did not prevent him from leading a normal life. He was apprenticed as a mechanic and in 1958 he obtained a job as a fitter and diesel engineer with the Gambia Produce Marketing Board. This organisation is responsible for the purchase and processing of groundnuts in the Gambia, and while working there Momodou Njie became thoroughly familiar with the operation and maintenance of diesel engines.

In 1979 Momodou Njie had a further attack of the same eye disease that had afflicted him so many years before and, as a result, lost the sight of his remaining eye. He was no longer able to work with the Gambia Produce Marketing Board and his employment had to be terminated. By this time he had two wives and seven children, so it was vital for him to find a new source of income to replace the salary that he had earned before.

Momodou Njie realised that it would be very difficult for him to get a job with anybody else, and he decided to start a business on his own. He recognised that he had a particular skill in diesel maintenance and decided that the best way he could make use of this to support himself would be to purchase a grain milling machine and to install it in Kaur in order to provide milling services to the community. He thought that this would be an ideal business since there was no similar service in the town and he would be providing a valuable social service with no competition, as well as making the best use of his mechanical skills.

Momodou Njie therefore approached the Social Welfare Department, which is the government organisation responsible for assisting disabled people to provide themselves with basic needs such as shelter, food and any equipment they need to maintain their mobility. Independent charities are also compelled to channel their assistance to handicapped and disabled people through this agency.

It was fortunate for him that the British Royal Society for the Blind was at the time of his application anxious to help blind people who had ideas for business and wanted to become self-reliant. The Society had made a revolving loan fund available to the Gambia Society for the Blind. This fund was disbursed to blind people through the Social Welfare Department on the basis of one-third grant and two-thirds loan.

Momodou Njie applied for 12,000 dilasis (US\$1 = D6.53) and his application was approved; he received a grant of D4,000 and a loan of D8,000. Since the Social Welfare Department had no expertise in assisting people to start businesses, Momodou Njie was referred to the Indigenous Business Advisory Services (IBAS), a government agency that gives business advice and consultancy services to small enterprises in the Gambia.

Momodou Njie discussed his business proposal with the IBAS and they agreed that it was viable, but they suggested that he would need a further D4,000, making a total of D16,000, if his business was to get off to a good start. The IBAS was able to provide a loan of this additional amount through a scheme that it operated in conjunction with the Gambia Commercial and Development Bank, funded by the United Nations Capital Development Fund.

Momodou Njie was now able to start his business. He purchased a diesel-operated milling machine, had it installed at his home in Kaur and started operations with the assistance of one employee. From the outset his business was very successful and he was able both to support all his family and to pay off the total of D8,000 that he owed within three years as scheduled.

In 1985, because his first venture had been so successful, Momodou Njie decided to expand his business. He borrowed a further D17,000 from the Gambia Commercial and Development Bank and bought a second diesel-operated milling machine. This was a portable installation which could be carried around from one village to another on a horse-drawn cart. This machine operates mainly in Farafenni,

Momodou Njie checking the operation of his grain mill

the second city of the Gambia, and a village called Keir Enderi which is on the border between the Gambia and Senegal. Both these towns are very busy because of the border traffic, and Njie's second machine was even more successful than the first. He has almost finished paying off the loan of D17,000 with which he bought it.

Momodou Njie employs two people, one to operate each of his machines. He himself travels from one machine to the other, collecting the receipts and monitoring the operations. He has acquired a great deal of experience in his business in addition to his initial training with the Gambia Produce Marketing Board, and feels that his employees cannot cheat him. He provides them with the necessary diesel fuel and knows exactly how much money they should be able to earn for each litre they consume. He has developed a remarkable ability to detect minor problems merely by listening to the machine, and can repair them right away himself. When there are more important problems, he hires a mechanic but can still provide expert guidance himself.

When they are in good running order the machines operate seven days a week. The average gross income per year is approximately D43,000 and after paying for fuel and lubricating oil, the wages of his employees and the rent of the places where he operates, as well as withdrawing approximately D20 a day for his family, Momodou Njie still earns a profit of approximately D15,000 per year. Because he has limited the amount he has withdrawn, Momodou Njie has reinvested almost D60,000 in his business since he started operating, as well as repaying the loans from the Gambia Commercial and Development Bank and from the Social Welfare Department.

One thing that Momodou Njie cannot do because he is blind is keep his own books. This service is provided to him free of charge by the Farafenni field officer of the IBAS. Thanks to this service, Momodou Njie feels that he is in close control of the finances and operations of his business and plans in the future to expand still further. He has few major problems, but he often finds it difficult to get spare parts for his milling machines and the diesel engines and sometimes has to go as far as Kaolack, in neighbouring Senegal, in order to buy what he wants. His blindness does not prevent him from making this trip and he is in no way discouraged.

He plans next to go into the production of seed oil. He has already bought two small groundnut processing machines and is working out his plans so that he can start this new enterprise in the near future, building on the sound basis he has already established.

Commentary: Group I

The four enterprises described in the foregoing case studies are all still dependent to a greater or lesser extent on outside assistance. The Jerusalem Co-operative and the Oyugis Sheltered Workshop clearly rely very heavily on external support; it may be that neither of them, and particularly the Kenyan group in Oyugis, is seriously expected by its sponsors or its members to become independently viable. Luwo Jambo attempted to become independent, but realised that his business would never become fully viable. He has now come back for further assistance in the hope that he can succeed the second time with the aid of more capital.

Momodou Njie, the miller from the Gambia, clearly runs the most successful enterprise of the four which have been described. He still depends on the Indigenous Business Advisory Service for bookkeeping services, but the case study gives the impression that he is fully capable of making use of the information he receives from his accounts. He requires assistance because he is blind, but he is able to analyse the data, make operating decisions and plan the future of his business based on the information provided by the IBAS.

The members of the Oyugis Workshop, through their committee, are nominally in charge of their enterprise. However, it appears actually to be under the direction of the adviser who is not one of the disabled members but an outsider appointed and paid for by an external agency. The members have come together in order to seek self-reliance, but they are effectively employees of the assistance organisation without an effective leader of their own. The administrator appears not to take the interest in the business that would be expected if it were his own, and although the present situation of the members is clearly preferable to total idleness there is little indication that they can ever become genuinely independent under the present arrangements.

Each of the other three case studies illustrates important characteristics which often distinguish entrepreneurs, whether disabled or not, from people who are more likely to seek employment with others. These characteristics have helped all three disabled entrepreneurs to reach their present position and should, if they are not diverted by well-meaning external advice, enable them to succeed in the future.

The most obvious characteristic, which numerous studies have shown to be perhaps the most vital attribute of entrepreneurs of any kind, is persistence. Sister

Mary of the Apostolic Faith struggled for years on her own in spite of wretched results and appears likely to be equally willing to persist in her efforts to encourage the members of the Jerusalem Co-operative to devote more time to their enterprise. Luwo Jambo has displayed perhaps the most remarkable persistence; he walked the hundreds of kilometres from his home to Harare with only a rubber pad to protect the stump of his amputated foot; he worked as a gardener and then as a cook for the same employer for 20 years, educating himself and learning a new skill at the same time, and then struggled for years at two separate centres in an attempt to establish his shoe repair business. Even now, he is not discouraged and is prepared to try again. Momodou Njie, like all people who have successfully overcome disability, was not discouraged by the loss of one eye nor even when he lost his sight altogether. Redundancy alone is enough to crush some people; Momodou Njie lost both his job and his sight, but still went on to start and run an expanding and profitable business.

All three people were also opportunists in the best sense of the word. They made the best use of their own skills and of whatever assistance was available, whether from family, or charitable or official sources. They grasped whatever opportunities the market provided and typified in their response to their problems the classic entrepreneur who "sees opportunities where others see problems".

They also displayed a remarkable ability to learn new skills quickly and to compensate for their disability by outstanding capacity in other ways. Sister Mary Gwande learned to be an excellent seamstress in two months, Luwo Jambo learned the art of shoemaking in his spare time after being a gardener and a cook, while Momodou Njie, in many ways perhaps the most remarkable of the three, seems to have developed a most unusual ability to diagnose and repair diesel motors through the use of sound and touch alone.

The case studies also have important implications for those who work to assist disabled people to become entrepreneurs. The Jerusalem Co-operative may be a small success for the 19 members who are not disabled and possibly for the other three disabled members apart from its leader and initiator, Sister Gwande herself. From her point of view, however, it could be argued that if she had been able to obtain some modest assistance as an individual in order to overcome her inability to market her own goods, she might have succeeded in establishing a viable tailoring concern. The IBAS, by contrast, realised the need to "fill the gap" by providing bookkeeping services in order to make up for Momodou Njie's blindness, and thus played an important part in his success.

The Oyugis group, like the Jerusalem Co-operative, appears to have come together in order to take advantage of government assistance. There are many good political and practical reasons why governments and other agencies find it more attractive to work with groups than with individuals, but in Sister Mary's case certainly, and possibly in the Oyugis situation, it might have been better if assistance had been available to people who wanted to work on their own as well as to groups. Like so many disabled people, such as Luwo Jambo, Sister Gwande and one or more of the Oyugis group, they might eventually have trained and employed other disabled people to work with them. This might have been less dramatic and slower, but would probably have provided a sounder basis for genuine future independence, albeit for a smaller number of people.

As so often happens, the assistance agencies appear to have neglected the importance of effective marketing. The Government's efforts to obtain school uniform contracts for the Jerusalem Co-operative were far from successful, and there appears to be a real risk that if Luwo Jambo is encouraged to restart his shoemaking business by a loan or grant to buy new materials and equipment, this will not in itself solve the basic marketing problem which he has so rightly identified. Momodou Njie with his mobile milling machine demonstrated that it is necessary for a business to reach out to customers rather than relying on them to come to the business. Disabled business people have to do this just as much as any others.

Assistance agencies, which are so used to people coming to them, have to remember that they must not only reach out to their clients but also assist their clients in turn to reach out to their customers. Any service, whether it be milling, shoemaking, tailoring or assistance for disabled entrepreneurs, has to be effectively marketed to its clients at the place and at the time where they need it.

Group II: Enterprises which received assistance

Babu Suryawanshi's dairy farm

Babu Suryawanshi was born in 1961 in Sangli district of Maharashtra State in India. He completed seven years of primary education and like most of the people in the district shared in his family's work and their modest income by working on their smallholding.

When he was 20 years old, Babu Suryawanshi was found to be suffering from cancer. As a result, his left leg had to be amputated above the knee. He had always been an active young man, and this seemed to be the end of the road. He had no motivation to do anything and might thereafter have withdrawn from society and become entirely dependent on his family.

Fortunately, Babu Suryawanshi was then sent to the local rehabilitation centre of the Indian Cancer Society. When he arrived, he was equipped with an artificial limb which went some way to restoring his mobility, but he still felt depressed and lacked the enthusiasm to do anything for himself. The staff of the centre had long counselling sessions with him, and they eventually succeeded in helping him to recover from the shock of his disability and to take an interest in his own future.

Because he had had some experience in agriculture, the staff of the centre advised him to take up dairy farming and worked out a detailed plan whereby he would be able to support himself by rearing cows. He was trained intensively in the necessary aspects of rearing dairy cattle and also received some simple management training so that he could keep the books and plan the financial aspects of his enterprise.

The staff of the centre then helped Babu Suryawanshi to obtain a loan of 10,000 rupees (US$1 = Rs.12.84) from the local branch of the State Bank of India, and they also arranged for him to receive a small grant of RS.700 from a fund maintained by the National Institute of Handicap Research in order to help him buy the initial supplies of fodder which he needed. He invested a further Rs.300 from his own savings and started his enterprise in April 1983, two years after the loss of his leg.

Babu Suryawanshi milking one of his cows

Babu Suryawanshi applied himself seriously to his business from the outset and now has four milking cattle. At the beginning he received some free outside help with keeping accounts and records for his business, and he also had a grant from the Cancer Society of Rs.1,233 per year for three years. This period expired in 1985, but by then Babu Suryawanshi was well able to manage and to expand his business by reinvesting the surplus he was earning in order to obtain further cattle. He sells approximately Rs.30,000 worth of milk every year and is left with a surplus of around Rs.11,000 after paying for the necessary fodder for his animals. He reinvests the surplus in expanding his small herd after he has repaid the scheduled instalments on his bank loan.

Babu Suryawanshi sometimes finds it difficult to obtain enough fodder for his cattle because it is in short supply in the area during times of drought, but this is a problem which affects all dairy farmers and he is not unduly discouraged by it. He has numerous plans for the future; he has received some training in poultry farming and hopes in the future to add this activity to his existing dairy enterprise. He also hopes to raise the necessary capital to install a bio-gas plant that will use the dung from his cattle and chickens to manufacture gas which he will sell to his neighbouring villagers for cooking. He reckons that he will need a total of Rs.5,000 to start his poultry enterprise and construct a bio-gas plant, and hopes to obtain a loan for this amount.

Babu Suryawanshi has, through his success, encouraged a number of his neighbours to obtain loans and start similar enterprises, although they are not disabled. He does not employ anybody directly but can legitimately take pride in the fact that 25 of his neighbours have so far succeeded in obtaining loans from the Government and are materially increasing their incomes partly as a result of being encouraged by his example.

The Rainbow Kiosk

To the ordinary uninformed passer-by, the Rainbow Kiosk is no different from any of the numerous refreshment parlours which serve snacks to people in the public plaza of Bacolod in the Visayas area of the Philippines. If you look closer, however, you can see that the signboard reads "Rainbow Kiosk, managed by the deaf". Beside it is a series of illustrations showing how the alphabet can be put over in sign language using the hands.

The Rainbow Kiosk was set up in October 1980 largely at the initiative of the local branch of Soroptimist International in Bacolod City, which wished to do something for the deaf people of the area. The members made a donation of the initial capital that was necessary to construct the kiosk, and they also succeeded in persuading the management of a local soft drinks factory to make an interest-free loan in order to finance the fitting out and decoration.

The Soroptimist Club in Bacolod is heavily engaged in a variety of forms of assistance to disabled people, and a small nucleus of deaf people were trained for two months in the simple management, budgeting and other skills which are necessary to run a food kiosk successfully.

A total of 11 people now work in the kiosk; eight of them are deaf, one has been disabled by poliomyelitis, one suffers from patch disease, and one is non-disabled. Three of the 11, two brothers and one sister, are all from one family and they are all deaf. The average age of the members is 25 years and they all work on a part-time basis; seven of them combine this work with attending elementary school, two are at high school and two have already gone on to college.

A view of the Rainbow Kiosk

The kiosk is open from 9 a.m. to 8 p.m., seven days a week. Each of the 11 members works for five half-days and one whole day a week and has one day off. The cashier, however, works for six days a week and has only one day off since it is more important that he should be on duty to handle the cash whenever possible.

Each of the members earns approximately 200 Philippine pesos (US$1 = P20.97) a month from the Rainbow Kiosk; this is barely enough to live on, but it makes a valuable addition to their incomes and supplements the support they receive from their families. Three of them also receive P200 a month in addition to their wage from some sponsors in the Federal Republic of Germany.

The snack foods which are sold by the Rainbow Kiosk are mainly obtained on consignment from a number of local suppliers, so the kiosk does not need to lay out working capital for stocks of its main products. Soft drinks, on the other hand, have to be paid for in cash but because of the rapid turnover and frequent deliveries this does not impose an undue strain on its finances. The Kiosk achieves an annual gross margin of something over P40,000, after paying for the cost of supplies, and when wages and other costs are deducted this leaves an annual profit of around P12,000.

The members finished repaying the loan from the soft drinks company some two years ago and the Rainbow Kiosk continues to expand its sales since it is one of the most popular places in the public plaza of Bacolod. The service is quick and friendly, and the prices of the snacks and soft drinks are more or less the same as those sold at the other kiosks. Many people go there out of curiosity, because they want to support the disabled people, or because they enjoy the friendly atmosphere of the place, which is the result of the effective way in which the members work together in the kiosk.

In spite of the fact that they are all still at school or college, all the members would prefer to work longer hours and to earn higher wages. This is not possible at the Rainbow Kiosk because the workload is not sufficient to employ them for more than the five half-days and one full day which most of them put in. They therefore hope that they can, some time in the future, put up another kiosk in some other part of Bacolod so that they can work more and increase their incomes.

Binti Manoa's dressmaking school

Binti Manoa comes from Itando, a small town in western Kenya. She suffered from poliomyelitis when she was a child and since then, as a result, she has been unable to walk.

When Binti Manoa left school she entered the Itando Rehabilitation Centre and was trained in tailoring for a period of 18 months. She did not receive any management training, but she was intelligent enough to realise that it would be difficult for her to obtain employment as a tailor because of her immobility. The alternative, which was the obvious one for somebody in her position, was to start up in business as a tailor on her own. However, she realised that it would be very difficult to travel every day to a market-place or some other location where people would be willing to come in order to have garments made by her. In the circumstances, she decided that the best thing to do would be to satisfy the demand for tailoring training from other people who did not suffer from disabilities and could therefore obtain jobs or set up as independent tailors, options which seemed to be very difficult for herself.

Binti Manoa was provided with a sewing-machine free of charge when she left the Itando Training Centre, and she started her sewing training school in September 1983 in a very small way. The Government, through the rehabilitation centre, provided her with rent-free premises which were worth approximately KSh400 a month, and she established her business there, initially with the one sewing-machine which she had received on completion of her training. She had received some training in fashion design as well as dressmaking, and she is a skilled seamstress, designer and business woman. As a result of her efforts, she has now been able to buy three more sewing-machines out of the accumulated profits from her business and she hopes in the future to be able to expand still further.

Miss Manoa is now able to train four people at a time; she charges Ksh100 for an hour of instruction, and Ksh150 for two hours. The trainees bring their own materials which they work on for training purposes and can then take away, either for their own use or for sale if they are up to the necessary standard.

At the present time, only Binti Manoa herself is employed in her school, and she pays herself a wage of Ksh200 a month. The total annual revenue from the training is approximately Ksh 34,000, and she has to spend some 14,000 shillings a year on maintenance of the machines, security and haberdashery items such as thread, buttons and needles.

The business is thus making a profit of around Ksh20,000 a year, after Binti Manoa's own modest wage, and she plans to continue reinvesting the profits in expansion. She aims in the future to buy more machines and to purchase her own permanent building for the school rather than relying on the Government's generosity. She would also like to be able to assist other disabled people by training them and encouraging them to do as well as she has, either by setting up schools in other areas or by working together as tailors on a factory basis.

Fely Lucas: pavement vendor

Fely Lucas lives in Cotabato City in the south of the Philippines. When she was 2 years old she contracted polio and has ever since been confined to a wheelchair. In spite of her disability, she was married at the age of 15 and had three children.

In 1973, when she was 23 years old, disaster struck Fely Lucas for the second time. Her husband died, and she was left with three children aged 4, 6 and 7 years. The double misfortune of widowhood and disability, together with the heavy responsibility of bringing up three young children single-handed, might have overwhelmed many people but Fely Lucas realised that she had to do what she could.

She had some experience in pig-rearing and sometimes earned a few pesos by castrating pigs for other people. She therefore decided to start a pig-rearing business and continued this for some time near her home, some 25 kilometres from the centre of Cotabato City. This business was not a success, however, and never earned enough money to sustain her family, so Fely Lucas then opened a *sari-sari* store, which is a very small general shop selling all kinds of things, such as kerosene, charcoal, confectionery and cigarettes, to people in the neighbourhood. This business

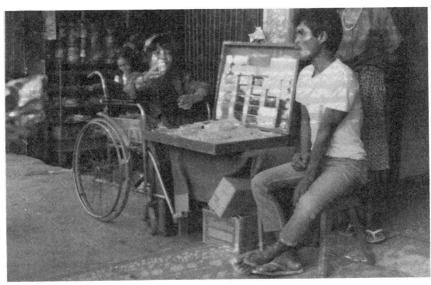

Fely Lucas, vendor of cigarettes and confectionery, in her permanent place of work — a pavement on one of the city's streets

was reasonably successful in a very modest way, but Fely Lucas was then forced to move to another house in the same area which had no facility for a *sari-sari* store. Her second effort at self-sufficiency was thus also unsuccessful.

Fely Lucas then decided that she would try to take advantage of the far larger number of potential customers in the central area of Cotabato, although it was so far away from her home. She took the remaining stocks of cigarettes and confectionery and became a pavement vendor in 1983.

She was at this time almost destitute but managed to secure a small loan of P500 from the Ministry of Social Services and Development. This tided her over the difficult initial period while her business found its feet and now, four years later, she has achieved a reasonable level of success. Sales amount to some P9,000 every month, and it costs her about P7,000 to buy the goods that she sells. This leaves a margin of some P2,000 a month and after paying her other expenses, which are mainly for transport, Fely Lucas is left with a profit of some P800 a month.

The total of just under P10,000 per year is a very modest amount on which to bring up a family of three children, but Fely Lucas feels that she can take pride in the fact that her two older children both managed to complete high school and her youngest daughter went on to college and is now in her second year. Fely Lucas now has five grandchildren and feels that in spite of everything she has so far succeeded in overcoming the enormous difficulties which faced her when her husband died 14 years ago.

Although she has almost finished educating her children, Fely Lucas has no shortage of plans for the future. She hopes to save or otherwise acquire enough capital to start up her pig-raising business again. She would also like to be able to invest some money in modifying her house so that she could once again open up a *sari-sari* store further to supplement her income.

Her main goal, however, has been inspired by the great difficulty she has every day in travelling from her home to the centre of Cotabato City and in returning at night. Because of her disability, the *jeepneys,* or small private buses which are used for transport in the Philippines, are reluctant to pick her up. Fely Lucas can understand this because it takes so long for them to load her wheelchair into the *jeepney* and then to unload it at her destination. Fely Lucas therefore wants to buy her own *jeepney*. This would be a major investment, but in addition to allowing her to travel more easily to the centre of the city, it would also, she thinks, be possible for her to hire a driver and to make money out of the vehicle while she was at work. It could then take her home in the evening, and she would thus at the same time solve her transport problem and further augment her meagre income.

Bob Sabio and Sons: Figurines

Bob Sabio was born in 1936 in Bacolod City in the Philippines. He was employed as regional supervisor for the Eternit Corporation, a branch of a multinational company that deals with water systems and also supplies building materials.

When he was 37 years old, Bob Sabio had to have an operation on his thigh and complications set in. As a result, he became a paraplegic and could no longer continue working with the Eternit Corporation because he was unable to move around easily.

A friend knew of his plight and introduced him to the idea of making plaster figurines which are a popular product in the Philippines, particularly during festival periods. Bob Sabio took to this new activity with some enthusiasm and found that his earlier experience of working with plaster and other water-based building materials was of some value. He started on his own in 1968 working underneath his raised house and enjoying very much the creative aspect of his new profession.

As time went on, Sabio's products became more and more popular in spite of the fact that there were many competitors, and he found it necessary to expand his business by hiring additional people to work with him. In 1987, 21 years after starting, he employs 12 people, all of whom are members of his extended family. As a result, his business now supports eight households in addition to his own, and he has made a significant contribution to creating jobs in his neighbourhood.

Figurine making is a very labour-intensive activity, and the plaster which is used is not particularly expensive. Sabio sells approximately P20,000 worth of figurines every month, and the material for this costs only a little over P2,500. His other costs, such as finishing materials, packing and transport, amount to just over P1,200 a month, and thus he is able to pay something over P6,000 a month in wages, or over P500 for each of his 12 employees.

After paying his helpers, and financing the materials and all other expenses, Sabio's business is currently earning a profit of almost P10,000 a month. He is also continuing to receive a grant of P1,000 a year from the Negros Occidental Rehabilitation Foundation, although this is not a particularly significant amount to

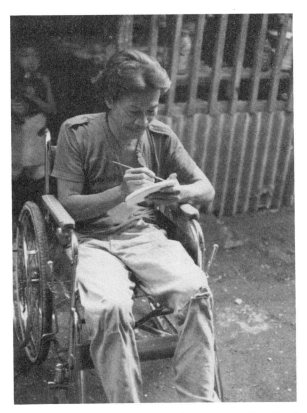

Bob Sabio putting finishing touches to one of his figurines; behind him is his makeshift shop

him at the present time. Bob Sabio has significantly improved his life-style, but he still lives in the low-income settlement where he was located when he started up. He feels that he could sell more figurines and further expand his business, thus employing more people, if he were to have a retail shop in the centre of the city. Sabio therefore hopes to accumulate the necessary capital both by saving the profits from his existing business and perhaps by borrowing more funds from outside, so that he will one day be able to realise his dream of having his own retail outlet.

Commentary: Group II

Although some of the five businesses described are still receiving modest external assistance, this is relatively insignificant in relation to their earnings. All of them, however, have benefited significantly from assistance of various kinds received earlier. We have attempted to present the case studies in a sequence of decreasing order of magnitude with regard to assistance. However much they have been helped, however, all the enterprises have relied mainly on the efforts and initiative of their founders, owners and managers.

Babu was clearly in desperate need when he lost his leg. The staff suggested what he should do, gave him the necessary training and arranged for finance from a bank. Their most important contribution, however, may have been the psychological encouragement they gave him when he was first admitted to the rehabilitation centre. Without this intensive counselling, it is doubtful whether he would have achieved anything at all.

One of the major distinctions between promoting self-employment for the disabled and assisting others who are not disabled may be that disabled people sometimes need this type of encouragement, as well as more familiar services such as training, advice and finance. It has already been pointed out that self-employment is not for everyone, and assistance agencies – even if they do not recognise this fact – are usually compelled by their shortage of resources to be very selective. They thus tend to select people who display initiative, have ideas, and are willing and able to demonstrate their commitment by obtaining information and generally participating in and taking over the process of setting themselves up in business.

Disabled people such as Babu may be different; he may indeed have possessed the qualities of enterprise before suffering the shock of cancer and amputation, but the staff of the centre had no way of finding out what he was like before this happened to him. All they could do was to offer him, and other patients, intensive counselling and encouragement in order to identify those who responded by coming out of their depression and taking control over their own lives.

Disability, like the loss of a secure job, unexpected bereavement, becoming a refugee or any other shock, can sometimes be the very stimulus that drives somebody to self-employment. Even if it were possible for rehabilitation staff to find out what sort of people their clients were before they were disabled, this would not necessarily be an accurate guide to their personalities afterwards. The experience may significantly enhance their energy, self-confidence and initiative or it may have precisely the opposite effect.

It is important to note that Babu, like most successful entrepreneurs, made some commitment to his enterprise from his own resources from the very beginning. He was not given or lent all the necessary money, but had to invest Rs300 from his own funds. Although this was a negligible amount compared with the total of Rs11,000 which he needed to start his dairy enterprise, it was probably significant in relation to his limited means. The rehabilitation centre helped him to make up the necessary amount by putting together a package from his money, their own small grant and a substantial loan from the bank. Assistance agencies must often recognise that their main function is to mobilise other resources rather than using their own. The Soroptimist Club of Bacolod helped the members of the Rainbow Kiosk with some funds, but it also used its contacts to persuade a private sector company to help and it no doubt facilitated the granting of rent-free space for the kiosk which was constructed with its money.

Disabled people are often even less able to obtain access to the authorities or to potential sources of assistance than are other marginalised groups because of their lack of physical and social mobility. The external agency that is able to help them bridge this gap can thus render a vital service which may be more useful than long-term financial assistance.

The rehabilitation centre gave Babu a regular supplement to his income, but only for three years. This was probably a very valuable cushion in the early years of his business, but it was rightly withdrawn when he showed that he was able to earn sufficient income from his enterprise without further subsidy.

Bob Sabio is continuing to receive P1,000 a year, or about US$50, although this is less than 1 per cent of the profits he earns from his figurine manufacturing enterprise. This small amount was probably very important to him at the beginning, and has of course been enormously devalued over the years by the effects of inflation. Nevertheless, it may be better for assistance institutions to follow the example of the rehabilitation centre of the Indian Cancer Society in Maharashtra and to cut off subsidies when they are no longer necessary. This enables the money to be spent on helping others to overcome the difficulties of starting on their own and also ensures that disabled people themselves recognise that their goal is to move beyond the needs of the subsidy.

Binti Manoa and Bob Sabio both showed how people themselves are often more able to come up with good ideas for self-employment than are outside advisers. Binti Manoa carefully appraised her own situation and the market, and selected a business for which there was a demand and which she could see would use her skills and avoid the problems posed by her disability. It is unlikely that any external adviser would have suggested making figurines as an enterprise and this is the kind of activity for which "project profiles" and similar pre-prepared studies are manifestly inappropriate. However, Bob Sabio's enterprise is probably the most successful so far described. Like any entrepreneur, he was alive to opportunities and picked up the idea with enthusiasm when it was suggested to him by his friend.

It may sometimes be necessary, as in the case of Babu, for an adviser to suggest what some people should do if they have no ideas of their own. The staff of assistance agencies must recognise, however, that their own ideas are unlikely to be as good as those which people have for themselves. The most carefully researched "project", suggested to and undertaken by an unenthusiastic entrepreneur, is unlikely to succeed as well as an apparently foolish or unconsidered idea implemented by someone who believes in it because he thought of it himself.

Like all the subjects of the case studies, Fely Lucas displayed remarkable persistence and resilience in the face of continued difficulties. It is interesting and typical of classic entrepreneurial behaviour that she still wishes to continue and indeed expand her activities although her responsibilities for her children's education are more or less completed. She has all kinds of other plans and successful business achievement has become an aim in itself rather than a means of increasing her income for the benefit of her children.

Many of the disabled business people covered by our inquiry expressed a desire to help other disabled people achieve independence through self-employment. Some may want to do this before they themselves have reached the stage where they can afford to help others or where they have anything worth showing in terms of an example. It may also be a standard response to interviewers, but the effective collaboration of the Rainbow Kiosk group showed that even people who suffer from a variety of disabilities are able to work together more effectively than many who do not suffer any common hardships.

Perhaps the most encouraging evidence in favour of self-employment for the disabled is Bob Sabio's statement that he is now happier than he used to be when he worked as a salaried employee, even though he had a senior job and was not disabled. Self-employment has provided him with an opportunity to obtain self-fulfilment in terms of personal creative self-reliance and support for his family; this is surely as much as anyone could ask.

Group III: Independent entrepreneurs

José Ocasla: Watch repairing

José Ocasla comes from La Trinidad, Benguet, an agricultural centre in Luzon in the Philippines. He was born in 1946 and when he left school he went into business as a rice trader. He purchased rice from traders in and around his home area, took it with him to Manila, which is also on the island of Luzon, and sold it there in the urban market.

This was a cash business and on his return trips to La Trinidad, he necessarily had to carry quite large sums of money in order to purchase more rice for the next journey. In 1968, when he was 22 years old, he was held up by robbers on one of his trips home from Manila and in his effort to defend himself he received several stab wounds, the most severe of which reached his spinal column and left him disabled.

José was admitted to the National Orthopaedic Hospital and stayed there for a total of one year. While he was there, he realised that it would not be possible for him to start up his rice trading business again because he could not move around.

José Ocasla has his watch repair stand at the back of his apartment

He therefore took advantage of a course in watch repair which was offered in the hospital and learned this at the same time as undergoing occupational therapy.

In 1969 José was discharged from hospital; his wife, who used to be a schoolteacher, took over the rice trading business as best she could, while José started up a watch repair business using the skill he had learned in the hospital. He fitted out a small workshop in the backyard of their apartment and started operations a little more than a year after he had been injured.

He invested P2,500 in the minimum necessary tools and his wife and other friends made it known in the area that he was offering a watch repair service. Because he works in a residential area, his business attracts very few casual customers, but he has, over the years since he started, maintained a small but steady flow of business. His annual sales are presently around P18,000 and he has to pay around P2,000 for the various materials he needs. This leaves a balance of only P16,000, and José reckons that it costs him over P2,000 a month to maintain his family; fortunately, his wife is still continuing the rice trading business in a small way and between them they manage to support themselves and their 16-year-old son.

Although this income is so much lower than he was used to earning through rice trading, the family is relatively well off when compared with the average level in the Philippines, but José cannot help comparing his present situation with that as a rice trader.

Lamin Sambou: The tailor

Lamin Sambou was born in 1949 in the village of Bajeh Senkerr in the Casamance region of southern Senegal. He was an active little boy and used to work on his family's farm and drive the cattle out for grazing with the other children.

When he was 8 years old, there was an immunisation campaign in Bajeh Senkerr and everybody was given an injection. Lamin had his injection in his right leg; the next morning when he tried to get out of bed, he found that he could not stand on the leg. His family did their best to get treatment, but without success; as a result, Lamin was thereafter disabled.

Because he could no longer participate in his family's farming activities, he went to live with his grandfather who was the village tailor. In spite of his disability, he retained his curiosity and active mind and was always watching his grandfather at work. Little by little, he learned how to cut out garments and to sew them and was able to help out his grandfather from time to time.

In 1965, when he was 16 years old, Lamin decided to start as a tailor on his own. Because he had no capital he hired a sewing-machine and continued in this way for two years. He then moved to Dakar, the capital city, where he lived with his uncle and carried on his business as a tailor. He stayed in Dakar for six more years and became quite skilled in sewing modern clothes. In 1973, although he was earning just enough to pay the rent for his small shop and the machine, and to make a modest living, he decided to return to the Casamance because living in Dakar was so expensive.

Lamin Sambou, working at his hand-operated sewing-machine

On his return home, his mother gave him a cow; he sold this for 1,500 CFA-francs (US$1 = CFA-Fr.300) and bought his first sewing-machine with the proceeds. He then moved from Bajeh Senkerr to Ziguinchor, the largest city in the Casamance, and worked there as a tailor for four years. His business prospered at this time and he bought four sewing-machines of his own. He hired and trained several workers and apprentices at this time, but in 1977 his health started to deteriorate and his business suffered at the same time. Until then he had been using a foot-pedal sewing-machine which he operated with his left leg. Unfortunately, the paralysis spread now to his left leg as well, but since sewing was his only trade, he had to persist; he sold two of his treadle-operated machines and bought a hand sewing-machine so that he could carry on.

He decided at this time to seek a change of scene and moved to Serrekunda on the outskirts of Banjul, the capital of the Gambia. This is only a few kilometres from Ziguinchor and at first his business was very slow. He then realised that he would do better if he was located in the middle of the city and he therefore moved to the centre of Banjul early in the 1980s. He has been working there ever since and his business is now reasonably successful.

Lamin has two sewing-machines, his own which is hand-operated and another treadle-operated one which is used by a colleague who is a qualified tailor and started as Lamin's apprentice. They have been working together for eight years now; Lamin does not charge his partner any rent for the machine, but in return, when Lamin has more work than he can handle, his partner does it for him without charge. At other times, his partner is free to use the machine for his own customers.

Lamin also has a young apprentice of 14. He runs errands and does some of the simple work such as ironing, folding and displaying the finished clothes. He is not paid a regular salary, but receives his meals and a gratuity of D2.5 a day.

Lamin, on average, earns a gross income of some D80 per day; something over D30 goes on supplies such as charcoal for the iron, threads, buttons and lining material, and another D7-8 per day are spent on rent, maintenance of the sewing-machines, and so on. Lamin says that he takes a further D28 per day, on average, for the upkeep of his own family, and this appears to be sufficient for his needs; like most Senegalese who live in the Gambia, he sends money home to his family from time to time.

Apart from the difficulty of obtaining spare parts, Lamin has no major problem with his business. But because he has been doing it for so long and the physical effort is very tiring on account of his disability, he would really prefer to do something else. He has a vague idea of starting to copy and sell music tapes, but if he ever does this he hopes to retain his sewing-machines and employ other tailors to operate them so that he will earn additional income from this source as well.

Agripa Mutetsa's watch repairs

Agripa Mutetsa was born in 1937 in a rural area of what is now Zimbabwe. He was physically disabled from birth with a deformed backbone and restricted growth, but he nevertheless completed six years of primary education.

When he had finished his schooling, he realised that he could not work on his family's smallholding and spent six years moving from one town to another looking for employment. Although Standard 6 was at that time considered to be a high level of academic achievement, his disability always prevented him from finding a job. He might have become a teacher, but his parents could not afford to pay fees for him to go to college; his qualifications would have secured a place in the police force, but he was not tall enough to be admitted and although he was quite capable of working in an office, most employers then, and indeed now, had a negative attitude towards disabled people.

Mutetsa realised that he would probably have to become self-employed in the end and thought of various ways of doing this; unfortunately, he could never accumulate any capital since he was living from hand to mouth on the generosity of his family and others, and he could see no way out of his dilemma. In 1960, by a stroke of luck, he got a job as a general handyman at a service station in Rafingora, some 65 kilometres away from his home. He was paid only Z$60 per month, but he decided right away to invest some of this in learning a trade so that he would no longer be dependent for employment on other people. He enrolled in a correspondence course on watch repair with the Mellkwark School of Watchmaking in South Africa, and in 1962 he passed the necessary tests and received his diploma. He immediately started work as a part-time watch repairer with the few tools he had been able to acquire and worked for two years in this way, continuing his job at the service station but also working during his free time and weekends at watch repair. There were few other watch repairers in the area and Mutetsa was able to earn enough both to buy all the necessary tools and to send some money to his parents.

In 1984 the Apostolic Church in Guruve, to which he had belonged since childhood, appointed him as a district secretary. This was a volunteer job, carrying no remuneration, but he did have to move to Guruve district centre in order to perform his duties. Mutetsa immediately gave up his job at the service station and moved to Guruve where he went into business as a full-time watch repairer. A fellow member of the Apostolic Church who owned a shop in the district centre was very happy to let Mutetsa operate free of charge on the veranda; by serving as a church dignitary, Mutetsa also attracted more customers to his own shop.

There was a lucrative market for watch repair, and in 1966, two years after he had moved to Guruve, Mutetsa found it necessary to recruit somebody to help him. He hired Mr. Peter, another disabled person, as an apprentice; for the first two years, Mutetsa paid Mr. Peter Z$60 a month, retaining Z$20 as a training fee, and after that he paid him a full wage of Z$80 a month. They worked together till 1977, by which time Mr. Peter was earning Z$150 a month; in that year they decided to split up and Mr. Peter moved to a farm some 25 kilometres away from Guruve to satisfy the customers who lived in that part of the district.

Mutetsa carried on working at the Guruve centre and by 1981 he was earning Z$35 a day because of the high demand for his services; people who lived in the area had previously had to travel a long distance to Harare or another town, and they were only too happy to have a competent watch repairer conveniently close to their homes. Mutetsa always maintained the highest integrity in his business as well as in his personal life; customers' watches were always repaired when Mutetsa said they would be, his charges were reasonable and the quality was high. His standing in the Apostolic Church enhanced his business success and the business also further enhanced his standing in the Church.

In 1981 Mutetsa's business fell back and his earnings were reduced to around Z$25 a day because of the inroads of electronic watches which he could not repair. He would very much like to learn how to repair electronic watches and has made inquiries about training facilities from the local community development workers. He has been informed, however, that it has so far been impossible to identify any institution which provides training of this sort.

Providing he can overcome this problem, Mutetsa would like to rent a space of his own in the market centre so that he could take on other disabled people and train them to achieve the same degree of independence that he has achieved. Because of the pace of technological change in watchmaking, however, it is doubtful whether he will achieve this in the foreseeable future.

Nazir Hakim's auto-rickshaw

Nazir Hakim was born in 1955 in Bombay, India. He completed four years of primary education and then persuaded a friend who owned a three-wheeled auto-rickshaw to allow him to use it during some of the time when the friend was resting.

In 1980 Nazir Hakim was diagnosed as suffering from cancer of the larynx and, as a result of the subsequent operation, he totally lost the power of speech. While he was in the hospital, he had obviously not been able to continue driving the auto-rickshaw, and when he was discharged he was so depressed by his inability to speak that he totally lost his confidence and felt unable to take up any activity.

Fortunately, Nazir Hakim was introduced to the local rehabilitation centre where a doctor trained him to speak without his larynx. The centre also had a programme for assisting disabled people to become self-employed, and because Nazir Hakim already knew how to drive an auto-rickshaw, it applied on his behalf for him to receive a priority allocation of an auto-rickshaw for his own use.

Nazir Hakim had by then gained sufficient confidence to apply to the bank for a loan; the total cost of the auto-rickshaw was Rs.28,500. He invested Rs.5,000 of his own, borrowed Rs.4,000 from members of his family and secured a loan of the balance of Rs.19,500 from the State Bank of India.

Nazir Hakim is now happily settled in his new enterprise; he earns approximately Rs.15,000 from taxi fares and has to pay out about Rs.6,000 for fuel, servicing, repairs and other charges. He is thus left with a surplus of some Rs.9,000 a year, which is sufficient for him to support himself and to keep up with the loan repayments to the State Bank of India.

This satisfactory experience with his business has still further enhanced Nazir Hakim's confidence; he now trains other people who have lost their voices in the skill of speaking without a larynx and provides a valuable example to those who suffer from similar disabilities. In the little spare time he has, he also carries out repairs on other drivers' auto-rickshaws, earning some further income for the support of his family. He has four children of his own, and he also has to provide some support for his elderly father and mother and his four brothers and five sisters. He is able to make a substantial contribution to their well-being and is generally satisfied with both his family and his business life.

Nazir Hakim's father has a small upholstery business and Nazir Hakim would like to enter this business himself. As a child, he had some experience in this field, and his present objective is to pay off his bank loan earlier than scheduled so as to be able to take out a further loan and go into the upholstery business as a supplement to his earnings from driving the auto-rickshaw.

Manuel Tan: Waysonics Radio/TV Tutorship

Manuel Tan from Bacolod in the Philippines contracted poliomyelitis when he was only seven months old. He has never been able to walk and depends entirely on his wheelchair to move around. As a child, it was very difficult for him to go to school but he nevertheless struggled on his own and successfully learned to read and write in both the local vernacular and English.

When he finished school, Manuel Tan enrolled on a correspondence course on electronics. He worked for some years repairing radios, televisions and other electronic items, but found this very difficult because of his lack of mobility. He knew from his own experience how difficult it was to obtain employment and was aware that education and training were perceived by the mass of the Philippine people as being an avenue to employment. He therefore decided to take advantage of this demand and at the same time to reduce his own need to move around by opening an electronics training school.

Manuel Tan therefore opened the Waysonics Radio/TV Tutorship, as he called his school, in 1970. He obtained a modest loan of some P500 from a friend in order to buy the minimum necessary equipment and has been operating his business ever since.

Waysonics now offers two basic courses, one in the repair and maintenance of electronic gadgets, including radios and amplifiers, and another which concentrates on colour televisions and videotape recorders. Both courses last for five months, during which the students attend a one-hour session five days a week. Tan can accommodate three groups of 20 students at a time, since he offers three one-hour sessions every evening, and he also offers early morning sessions when there is sufficient demand. The courses are strongly practical in their orientation, and the students are required to complete a number of "projects" involving the assembly of complete electronic devices. They provide their own components for most of these exercises and are then able to take away the completed assemblies for their own use or for sale. Waysonics does lend certain of the more expensive components for projects such as fire alarms or sirens.

Waysonics currently enrols some 80 students per year and each pays a fee of P1,500. This gives a total income of P120,000. Tan employs two part-time apprentices who receive just over P3,000 a year each, and the cost of course materials amounts to some P48,000 after paying other costs, utilities, and so on; a surplus of some P60,000 per year remains. The class-rooms and accommodation are especially adapted to electronic instruction and are worth approximately P350,000 at this time. Manuel Tan supports his wife and four children from the income he earns from the business, but has also obviously been able to reinvest substantial sums from the surplus in improved facilities.

Manuel Tan would like to expand still further, but is constrained by his own shortage of time and by the class-room space available. He hopes eventually to set up a full-scale electronics and technical school, accredited to the Ministry of Education, Culture and Sport. This would obviously be a major undertaking involving substantial sums, but there appears to be no reason why Manuel Tan should not succeed in this as well as he has in his business so far.

George Karasa: The Museka Butchery and General Store

George Karasa was born in 1938 in Guruve district of what is now Zimbabwe. As was common in those days, his primary education was spread over many years since the family often needed him to work in the fields. As a result, he did not finish his six years of primary education until he was 26 years old, and he then took a job with the national railways.

In 1975 his eyesight started to deteriorate and by 1979, when he was 41 years old, he became totally blind. At that time the railway company had no pension scheme for its lower-level employees, and although George Karasa was by that time married and had two children to support, he had to leave the city with only a few dollars in his pocket to return to his rural home with no apparent way of earning his livelihood.

During the next three years, George and his family went through a very difficult period, being totally dependent on members of his extended family who could ill afford even to keep themselves. Things were made even worse in 1982 when his wife deserted him, leaving the two children in his care.

At this point, George decided that he would try to reopen his father's butchery shop, which had been closed since 1978 when the War of Independence was at its peak. He persuaded his father to lend him Z$50 and the business was a great success from the very beginning. He employed the man who had worked for his father and within two years, by the end of 1983, he had accumulated profits of Z$15,000 which he invested in a general store.

This was a wise decision because an extended period of drought hit Zimbabwe at this time and it became very difficult to buy animals for slaughter since they were in poor condition and farmers were unwilling to sell them. His sales fell from one carcass a week to one carcass a month, but the general store was very little affected and was by 1985 earning an annual profit of some Z$5,000. At this time, the butchery was only earning a profit of about Z$400 a year, but the total was more than enough to pay a fair wage to his employee and to enable George to maintain a reasonable life-style for himself.

In spite of being blind, George knows where most of the goods in the store are kept and is able to serve customers since he knows his way around the shop so well. He can count out change and distinguish one note from another, but he relies on his younger brother, who is an accountant in Harare, for bookkeeping and assistance with financial management. His brother returns regularly to Guruve and prepares the books for George, and he is also able to check the cash and the stocks in order to make sure that nobody is taking advantage of George's disability.

George now employs two people in the butchery and one in the general store and enjoys a friendly but businesslike relationship with them. There is clearly a risk that his suppliers, employees or customers will take advantage of his blindness, but because he is well respected in the community, anyone who was tempted to steal from him would probably be discouraged by social pressure. He has also developed an almost uncanny familiarity with the stocks and with the general workings of the business and it appears that with his brother's regular visits, he is able to manage his two businesses as effectively as any sighted person.

Mang Tibong: Miniature musical instruments

Mang Tibong was born into a small farming family in Luzon in the Philippines in the late 1930s. At the age of 3 he contracted polio, and ever since he has only been able to walk with difficulty with the aid of a stick.

After he had finished elementary school, he found that it was impossible to make any useful contribution to farming on his family's smallholding, and he moved to the nearby city of Manila. After some time, he was successful in obtaining a job as a gardener with a wealthy family and he worked for them for some years. Although his family did not give him any financial assistance, they respected him for his commitment and hard work and always encouraged him to look for better ways of earning a living.

While working for the family, he came into contact with one of the staff of Philippine Crafts and was offered a job with this organisation. He worked for them for three years and became quite an expert in using woodworking machinery and in

Mang Tibong outside his miniature musical instrument factory

hand carving, and he then moved to another woodworking factory where he worked for a few months. He spent two or three years working with one factory after another in order to acquire new skills and in 1962 he decided, with the encouragement of some of the customers of his employer at the time, to go into business on his own.

He borrowed P250 from one of his brothers and started in a very modest way in his home in Quezon City (part of Metro Manila) hand carving miniature musical instruments from a variety of local timbers.

The business has expanded steadily since that time; Mang Tibong has now constructed his own factory, built on a site which he bought with the aid of a P300,000 loan from a commercial bank, and employs a total of 60 people. They manufacture miniature wooden models of virtually every musical instrument, including drums, violins, guitars, pianos, saxophones and innumerable others, and they are sold not only in the Philippines but also to export markets throughout the world.

Mang Tibong has participated in international trade fairs in South-East Asia, Europe and the United States, and he now has a small sales office in Los Angeles, managed by his eldest daughter, which handles his export sales to the United States and related markets.

The annual sales of the business amount to some P350,000; the timber and other materials cost P50,000, some P90,000 are paid out in wages and a surplus of about P150,000 is left after paying the other costs. Most of this is reinvested in the business and is used for paying off the bank loan. Mang Tibong has received a number of awards in recognition of his success. He is also a member of his village council and is director of vocational services for the local Rotary Club.

Mang Tibong employs only two disabled people in addition to himself, but his long-term objective is to enable far larger numbers of disabled people to share in his success. His plan is to build a sheltered workshop for the seriously disabled, under the auspices of a foundation, so that they can be trained in woodwork and can then either leave and go into business for themselves, as he has so successfully demonstrated, or can remain within the workshop and produce items for sale.

Mang Tibong feels that if he succeeds in achieving this ambition it will be a satisfactory culmination to the great progress he has made since he was an unemployed youth, hobbling round Manila looking for a job as a gardener.

Commentary: Group III

The foregoing case studies show that some disabled people are able to achieve a dramatic level of business success with little or no official assistance. They have so convincingly overcome their disability that they are far more successful than most entrepreneurs who have not had to labour under a physical handicap, as well as all the difficulties which affect anyone starting his or her own enterprise.

An attempt has been made to present these last case studies in ascending order of success. We started out with José Ocasla, whose watch repair business might appear very successful to some other people, but who is dissatisfied because it compares so unfavourably with the lucrative job which he enjoyed before he was disabled. Lamin Sambou, the Senegalese tailor, appears to be one of the few people whose physical condition has been a major problem since he started his business. Most of the entrepreneurs who are described became disabled either in childhood or later in life and their condition then stabilised. Lamin lost first the use of one leg and then the other, and although he has successfully changed to a hand-operated sewing-machine, the experience has clearly moderated his enthusiasm for tailoring.

The Zimbabwean watch repairer has successfully integrated his religious affiliation with his business, but technological progress threatens to destroy the basis of his enterprise. The last four case studies describe people who appear to have found personal fulfilment as well as economic independence through business ventures, and are also sharing their good fortune with others.

It may be coincidental that the most successful businesses, such as the miniature musical instrument factory, George Karasa's shops and the Waysonics Electronics School are those that have received the least outside assistance. None of the people described in this last set of case studies has been constrained by inappropriate assistance, like some of the earlier examples, but these last three do demonstrate quite clearly that some disabled people are able to achieve reasonable business success, by any standards, without receiving any help from outside their family.

One characteristic of many successful entrepreneurs is that they do not ascribe their success to luck or good fortune, but to their own efforts. Anyone who is disabled is very unlucky, by most people's standards, and George Karasa, for instance, lost his sight, his job and his wife in a short period. It might be suggested that he was "lucky" in that his father was willing to lend him Z$50 and that the empty butcher's shop was available, but these are scarcely dramatic examples of good fortune. Like all entrepreneurs, he made the best of whatever was available rather than blaming bad luck and doing nothing.

Both José Ocasla and Nazir Hakim owed their physical rehabilitation and the idea for self-employment through watch making and auto-rickshaw driving to the institutions which assisted them after they were disabled. They both made the best of these ideas and of the other facilities that were offered. Rehabilitation, whether it is combined with assistance for self-employment or not, involves a subtle process of gradual transfer of responsibility to the patient so that he or she eventually takes charge of the whole process. In the examples of Hakim and Ocasla, this process appears to have been effectively carried out. Hakim's case, in particular, demonstrates how self-employment is not only the result of enhanced confidence but also contributes significantly to it. It is not suggested that self-employment should be seen as a means to rehabilitation in that it is worth while even if the business fails. It is hard to imagine, however, more cogent evidence of rehabilitation than the ability to become self-supporting through self-employment. This demonstrates to the disabled person and to the world at large that the process is complete.

Family support, particularly in the early stages, was vital to all the people described. The extended family still plays a major role in most developing countries and compensates in part at least for the lack of institutionalised social security systems. Unlike professional social workers or disability benefits, family support is clearly attuned to the needs of the individual. It may indeed be ideal when the family and the institution combine to provide a complete package of support, such as that which was available to José Ocasla.

It is significant that four out of the five most successful of these entrepreneurs, that is Mutetsa, Hakim, Tan and Mang Tibong, not only intend but are already helping other disabled people by assisting with their training or by employing them. Official regulations which require organisations to hire a certain minimum proportion of disabled people are often honoured more in the breach than in the observance, and employers who are able-bodied often find it very difficult effectively to integrate disabled people into an organisation so that they can make a proper contribution. It is perhaps natural that those who are disabled themselves are more able to understand and thus effectively assist other disabled people, and it may be that some able-bodied people would be unwilling to work for a disabled boss.

Nevertheless, it is on the face of it paradoxical that disabled entrepreneurs, who have the possibility of hiring the most productive workers, in fact prefer to employ disabled people. This may be ascribed to sympathy in the genuine sense of suffering with someone and thus being able to understand and assist them effectively. It may also be that disabled people who have succeeded in re-establishing themselves through self-employment realise from their own example that disability does not necessarily mean low productivity. If they can earn their own living and support others when so many able-bodied people cannot, they may be right in selecting other disabled people to work with them purely on the basis of financial viability.

Note

[1] The exchange rates quoted in this book are those of December 1987.

4

What do disabled entrepreneurs need?

Problems of the disabled self-employed

The foregoing 15 case studies were drawn from a sample of 53 enterprises owned and run by disabled people. We have already emphasised that this is in no way a representative sample of all businesses of this type. It is interesting to observe, however, that when the entrepreneurs were asked to state what was the most pressing problem that faced them in their business, the responses were very similar indeed to those which able-bodied business people have given to the same question in innumerable surveys all over the world.

Their answers can be summarised as follows:

- shortage of finance   27
- too few customers   10
- other problems   8
- no problems   4
- shortage of raw materials   2
- health-related problems   2

The low figure for health-related problems is particularly significant. We have already observed that Lamin, the Senegalese tailor working in the Gambia, was the only example in the detailed case studies whose business appears to have suffered seriously because of health problems which arose after he had started.

The interviewers were all people involved in rehabilitation work so that they might have been expected to be more sensitive to difficulties arising from physical disability than to purely business problems, and the business people themselves would probably have been willing to mention health-related difficulties to interviewers with this background if such problems had been important. It is probable that many disabled people, and particularly those who have had the courage and persistence to become self-employed, regard their disability as part of their environment.

Problems before starting

It is important to recognise, however, that the respondents were all people who had succeeded in starting their own enterprises, even if they were only on a very modest scale. The answers, therefore, do not relate to the period before they started, but to the time of the interview when they were already in business. It would have been quite impractical to interview disabled people who wanted to go into business but had not yet succeeded in doing so, because there would have been no way of identifying them. Staff of rehabilitation centres and other readers of this book are probably more likely to be trying to assist people who want to become self-employed rather than those who have already succeeded, and we should therefore attempt to suggest what their problems might be.

The case studies in the previous chapter give some indications; in addition to the familiar problems of initial capital, markets, premises and so on, a number of disabled people who had made a success out of self-employment appeared to rehabilitation workers and, at least in retrospect, to themselves to be quite incapable of taking such a radical step. They totally lacked the confidence to regain any control over their own lives and would have appeared to be most unpromising material in any assessment of entrepreneurial potential.

The staff who helped people in this situation were doubly successful because they not only helped the disabled people to regain their confidence, but also assisted them on the way to economic independence. It is important, nevertheless, to stress yet again that it would be wrong for self-employment to be offered as a standard or even an ideal way to attain self-sufficiency. The objective must be to enable people to choose for themselves, in full knowledge of the advantages and the disadvantages and of what will be required of them. Disabled people often feel, and indeed often are, cut off from the world; entrepreneurs are people who grasp opportunities, but someone who is not exposed to opportunities can scarcely be expected to grasp them.

During the process of rehabilitation, therefore, every effort must be made to ensure that disabled people have the chance to be a part of the world outside the centre or institution and to observe the threats and opportunities which surround them. The majority of institutions that promote self-employment try to avoid giving people ideas. They ask people applying for loans, training or other assistance what kind of enterprise they want to start, and claim that people who have not had sufficient interest or enthusiasm to identify an idea are unlikely to demonstrate great entrepreneurial potential.

Some of the case studies suggest that this may not be an appropriate approach for disabled people since their lack of exposure to the world and their lack of confidence make it very difficult for them to put forward ideas themselves. In such a situation, the work of the counsellor should be to suggest the option of self-employment, together with the alternatives. The choice of self-employment and of what type must rest with the disabled person. Even if the counsellor finds it quicker or easier to obtain information about raw materials, markets, equipment, and so on, every attempt must be made to encourage the prospective entrepreneur to find the necessary information. This may be difficult, but it will be no more difficult than actually being self-employed. The experience of obtaining the information will be a valuable test of commitment and enthusiasm. If the prospective entrepreneur is discouraged by the experience and decides against self-employment, this can be a cheap and relatively harmless experiment which is far less damaging in economic and psychological terms than failure in business.

Shortage of capital

Shortage of capital was the most commonly mentioned problem by the disabled people in our survey who were already in business, as it is in every survey of this type. Disabled people are even more likely than most to lack the capital needed to start a business, however small in scale, and for this reason financial assistance is often a part of the assistance package.

When the entrepreneurs were asked to state the major source of their initial capital, their answers were as follows:

- obtained a grant   20
- used own money   13
- obtained a bank loan   11
- help from family   8
- no initial capital needed
  (handicraft)   1

The figure for grants is, as might have been expected, high given the large number of institutions which give grants rather than loans, as will be discussed in the following chapter. Most of the entrepreneurs who relied mainly on money from the family or on their own resources had had no training or other assistance. They are the genuinely "self-made" entrepreneurs, and it is certainly very difficult for anyone, particularly a disabled person, to obtain a start-up loan unless he or she has the support of a training institution or similar organisation. We saw in a number of the case studies, however, that one of the main contributions of some rehabilitation institutions is to make it possible for people to borrow money from a bank and thus to establish a relationship which might be expected to endure long after the enterprise has ceased to need regular support from the institution.

Marketing

The second most common problem of our entrepreneurs was a lack of customers; they were asked to state to whom they sold their products or services and their answers were as follows:

- direct to the general public   52
- to other disabled people   16
- to other businesses   13
- to assistance institutions   5
- to foreign customers   3

The total adds up to more than the 53 respondents because many sold to more than one type of customer. It is very encouraging to see that only one of our sample sells only to a sheltered market in that he sells catering services to the support institution which helped him to start. It appears that even in this case, his service is fully competitive and is bought not because he is an ex-trainee of the customer.

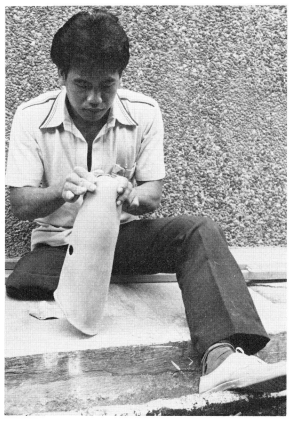

A disabled man in Indonesia making an artificial leg

All the others who sell to other disabled people also sell to the general public as well; it is often suggested that disabled people cannot compete in the open market and must therefore enjoy a sheltered market such as other disabled people who are themselves funded to buy from them by support institutions. There may be some advantages in terms of social solidarity and mutual support in promoting sales by disabled people's enterprises to other disabled people. Wheelchairs are typical products of this kind, and there are disabled people's co-operatives in the United Kingdom, the United Republic of Tanzania and elsewhere which make wheelchairs and other metal products of this kind for rehabilitation institutions, usually the ones with whom their members trained.

There is, nevertheless, a danger in this "closed cycle" type of system in that the disabled manufacturers are never exposed to the outside world and are necessarily forced to remain dependent on a support institution, even if they become fully able to satisfy its demand at an economic price. Rehabilitation must surely mean re-entry to the wider world; if a period of sheltered sales or a proportion of such sales is a necessary part of the re-entry process, this can be very effective, but total reliance on the sheltered market must be phased out if at all possible.

The fact that virtually all our respondents sold to the general public and only a minority sold to disabled people at all demonstrated quite clearly that even if the businesses are only marginal, people who are free to spend their money as they wish will buy goods and services from disabled people. Sympathy may play a part in this, although none of our case studies suggests that this was an important part of the marketing appeal of any of the businesses described, except perhaps for the Rainbow Kiosk in Bacolod; they seem to be providing goods and services in a competitive market at a price and of a quality that people want.

Other problems

A number of the disabled entrepreneurs operate their businesses in what might be considered inadequate locations. They may have been forced to do this because of their need to work from home, but their results suggest that they have shown definite business acumen in picking good spots which enable their customers to obtain their services more conveniently than before. At any rate, our sample of enterprises does not seem to need assistance with marketing as such; like most good business people the entrepreneurs would like more customers but are surviving on what they have and are in many cases taking steps to enlarge their market themselves.

It is difficult to judge the extent to which the businesses suffer from poor quality or design which might be remedied by training. Just over half the 53 business people had been trained in an institution, while a further third had been informally apprenticed to other businesses. The rest had received no training as such at all. Of those who had been trained, about half had been in training for a year or more. While it is certainly true that training is never complete in any trade and that people go on learning so long as they are working, it does not appear that more training would achieve useful results. As all except one of the entrepreneurs were able to sell on the open market, and there is no evidence that the exception could not have done so had he wished, it appears that their quality and prices are at least equal to or better than their competitors.

It may be, in fact, that some people are trained for longer than is necessary; "trainingism", as it has been called, is a common problem in many parts of the world when authorities act as though training and more training can solve every problem. There are some vocational training institutions working with carefully selected able-bodied people which offer full-time courses for two or even four years in skills such as carpentry or tailoring. It may be that someone who has been trained for two years is better than someone who has been trained for only one year, but the costs per trainee are so high that the benefits are inevitably restricted to very few people.

Disabled people may of course need more training than others, but it is hard to see why tailors and shoemakers, for instance, need over a year of full-time training. There are examples in the case studies of people, such as Sister Mary, the tailor, Luwo Jambo, the shoemaker, or Agripa Mutetsa, the watch repairer, who acquired a high level of skill in two or three months or entirely through part-time work by correspondence. If there is a heavy demand for training and resources are limited, it could be argued that shorter, better-organised training would be more equitable. Over-extended training may be a sign that institutions do not know what to do next.

One-third of the business people reported that they had received "some" management training; however, it is difficult to tell exactly what they meant by this. There is no data to suggest that these enterprises were more or indeed less successful than the others. The entrepreneurs were also asked whether the major management decisions in their enterprises were made by disabled people or by others. Although we tried to exclude sheltered workshops from our survey, many of the enterprises were receiving some regular management assistance from outside; nevertheless, only in one of the businesses were the major decisions said to be made by outsiders who were not disabled. There is no reason to suppose that management as such is particularly difficult for people who suffer from any form of physical disability, but these results indeed suggest that the disabled entrepreneurs actually run their businesses themselves. They are not "puppets" of support institutions, nominally independent but actually wholly dependent on management from outside. Although this should not be unexpected, it may surprise some people who believe that physical disability must inevitably involve at least some impairment of the ability to make independent decisions.

It appears, therefore, from both the case studies and the answers from the full sample of 53 businesses, that the needs of disabled entrepreneurs are not very different from those of other people who are in business for themselves, except that greater efforts may be necessary to rebuild their confidence at the initial stages. We should now look at the sample of rehabilitation institutions to see to what extent they are addressing the needs of the disabled people they are trying to help.

5

What is being done for disabled entrepreneurs?

Organisations and their funding

Our survey included 32 rehabilitation institutions which are involved, to some extent at least, in helping disabled people become self-employed. Seventeen of them are in India, ten are in Kenya, three in the Philippines, one in the Gambia and one in Zimbabwe, and a full list of the institutions which co-operated in the survey is given in Annex II to this book.

It was not possible to obtain any conclusive information as to the success or otherwise of the institutions in their efforts, and there is no reason to suppose that this group of organisations is any more representative of all such institutions than the 53 disabled entrepreneurs are representative of all disabled people who are in business for themselves.

It may, nevertheless, be of some interest to attempt to summarise their activities in this field in order to give some idea of the various ways in which they organise their work and to compare them with similar institutions in the same countries and elsewhere which are promoting self-employment for able-bodied people. We saw in the previous chapters that the needs of the disabled are not so very different from those of anyone wanting to start a business, except perhaps for the initial need for self-confidence. Are the institutions offering radically different programmes of assistance because their clientele are disabled and, if so, is this appropriate?

Twenty-one of the institutions surveyed were private voluntary organisations, while the remaining 11 were government departments. The sources of funding on which an institution relies are often a useful indicator of the way it may be expected to operate, and the following list summarises the sources from which these 32 institutions obtained the money to finance their operations:

- government only   11
- combined government and voluntary donations   11
- voluntary donations only   6
- voluntary donations and sales of goods   4

These figures show that in the Gambia, India, Kenya and the Philippines, at any rate, government recognises that voluntary organisations are often the most effective agencies through which to reach those in need; about half the voluntary organisations are partly funded by government and only a minority are wholly dependent on donations.

This approach is being used throughout the world in dealing with all manner of disadvantaged people, as governments come to realise that it is very difficult for their staff to match the commitment, flexibility, compassion and grass-roots contact of those who work for charities.

It is significant that the training institutions which stated that they depended to any extent on revenue from sales of products or services provided by their trainees are the only ones that are not receiving any funds from government. It is to be hoped that this does not mean that government support deprives agencies of the stimulus to earn money by selling their services since the discipline and quality requirements of the market-place are often an important part of successful vocational training.

Clients and the objectives of rehabilitation

All the institutions covered in the survey, except for the Indigenous Business Advisory Service (IBAS) in the Gambia, are rehabilitation institutions working only with disabled people so that our sample includes practically no vocational or self-employment training institutions which include both able-bodied and disabled people among their clients.

This one-sided concentration may be unfortunate but probably represents the reality of the recruitment policy of most vocational training institutions for the able-bodied; demand for places usually exceeds supply and any serious disability is almost certain to disqualify a candidate. Momodou Njie, the successful miller from the Gambia, benefited from the services of the IBAS only because he was referred by the Government's Social Welfare Department. It would appear that most disabled people must depend on specialised rehabilitation institutions for the training they need to become self-employed.

The admissions policies and overall objectives of the 32 institutions can be briefly summarised as follows:

Type of disability

All types of physical disability	22
Blind only	6
Deaf or blind only	1
Leprosy patients only	2
Cancer patients only	1

Proportion of trainees said to become self-employed

100 per cent	0
Over 50 per cent	10
11-49 per cent	7
Under 10 per cent	8
Not known	7

Number of trainees said to become self-employed each year

100 or more	3
21 to 99	3
11 to 20	4
6 to 10	4
Under 5	6
Not known	12

These figures suggest that most of the agencies operate on a rather small scale. Two of the three which produce over 100 self-employed ex-trainees each year do not have self-employment as their main objective, and the only really large institution specialising in training for self-employment is the Indian Cancer Rehabilitation Society, 85 per cent of whose trainees, numbering some 200 each year, start their own businesses. Like the other organisations which appear to be very large in terms of their numbers of trainees, they operate from a number of relatively independent branches.

Most of the government institutions are branches of a national network and it is encouraging to see that they operate on a local basis close to their clients and thus avoid the problems of large organisations which tend to serve only the urban minority. There are many economies of scale which might appear to be gained through expansion but the intangible disadvantages of bureaucracy, formality and "distance" – in every sense – from the clientele almost always outweigh them.

It is also significant that only a minority of the institutions stated that more than half of their trainees eventually become self-employed; the institutions are generally involved in training disabled people for whatever form of self-sufficiency eventually seems practical for them. This may be self-employment, but it may also be employment with others or employment within a sheltered workshop owned and managed by the rehabilitation institution itself.

Since the institutions accept trainees on the basis of their disability and not because they appear to have some special interest in or aptitude for self-employment, it would be quite wrong to direct people who are physically or, more important, emotionally unsuited for self-employment to try to start their own businesses. It should be stressed yet again that only a small minority of any population are actual or even potential entrepreneurs; there are reasons why disabled people may find this form of employment more attractive than others, but there are other reasons why they may not. Training institutions must show them what is possible, but must not in any way force them into it.

The possibilities for enterprise are unlimited, as we have already seen in the case studies. There does not appear to be any type of business which is particularly associated with any given kind of disability, except perhaps for massage with blindness in some Asian countries. However, any institution which works only with people who suffer from one kind of disability may fall into the trap of attempting to direct them into the same type of business.

It is therefore significant that only six of the 32 institutions work exclusively with blind people, and one with the deaf and blind, while a further three work only with leprosy and cancer patients, whose disabilities are of many different kinds. The remaining 22 institutions work with the complete range of disabilities and are thus unlikely to concentrate on one type of business because they believe it is the most suitable one for their clients.

The training offered

The following list summarises the skills in which the institutions offer training:

- Various trades   27
- Vending only   2
- Carpentry only   1
- Handicrafts only   1
- Weaving only   1

It is interesting that most of the institutions do not specialise in any particular type of training. It is all too common for vocational training institutions to be "facility driven" in that they train people in the particular skills for which they have the equipment and the instructors, rather than in the skills which their clients want and for which there is a demand in the market-place. Although the particular trades may have been chosen because there was a need for people with those skills at the time the course was started, scarcity of anything is likely to be followed by a surplus as large numbers of institutions and individuals respond to the demand. Many vocational training institutions are thus training people in skills for which there is little or no demand. Disabled people who have been trained in such institutions are even less likely than the able-bodied to find a job or to start a successful enterprise of their own.

Two of the institutions, both operating in India, specialise in training people to be vendors. It is very unusual for people to be trained in an institution as vendors or petty traders, or hawkers as they are often called. This is generally viewed as an "unproductive" activity, which is in some way not as legitimate as manufacturing or services; most governments are more concerned to limit and control the numbers and location of vendors than to assist more people to start this type of activity.

It is in fact just as "productive" to add value to products by making them available in the right quantities and at convenient times and places as it is to add value by physically changing raw materials into finished products. It also generally requires less capital since little or no equipment and less specialised skills are needed. The skills that are needed are also more transferable to different types of product than are manufacturing or servicing skills; Agripa Mutetsa's watch repair business, for instance, may fail because his skill cannot be applied to electronic watches. If he had been selling rather than repairing watches, he could have changed from clockwork to electronic watches with little difficulty.

Vending is clearly the most common form of self-employment for the disabled, as it is for everyone who has to rely on the so-called "informal sector" to survive. Only just over a fifth of our sample of self-employed people were vendors, but this sample was obviously biased in favour of people who had benefited from training. A truly random survey of self-employed disabled people would almost certainly show that the vast majority are in fact traders, and our case studies give no reason to suppose that vending is any more or less remunerative than other forms of enterprise.

Petty trading is certainly easier to enter than manufacturing or services and it may be that more effort should be devoted to helping disabled people to start trading businesses. One generally accepted maxim for development of any sort is that the intervention should "start where the people are". Many disabled people are already vendors and many more might be helped to become successful in this field if more training institutions accepted its legitimacy.

Those who are responsible for institutional training programmes are often tempted to extend the duration of the courses they offer, which inevitably means that less people can be trained given the same resources. The following figures show that our 32 institutions do not appear to have fallen into this trap.

Duration of training

- Under one year   11
- One to two years   11
- Over two years   7
- No training courses   3

Among the institutions providing the longest courses are those which specialise in training for the blind, one in India and the other in Kenya. In addition, five of the seven institutions whose training lasts more than two years are in fact employing the majority of their trainees in sheltered workshops, so that they are not actually self-employed.

The great majority of the institutions which train people for genuine self-employment are therefore completing the training is under two years. This compares favourably with most training for the able-bodied, which often lasts for a full two years and even longer. The costs of such training are enormous in comparison to the added earning capacity which is attained by the trainees, particularly if foreign assistance is involved, and the numbers who can be trained are thus inevitably reduced.

Very long periods of training may be needed in order to enable people to reach the standards required by official trade certificates, which are often of foreign origin. Although these qualifications are often not very relevant to the requirements of later employment, they are still in many cases the condition for entry into the formal labour market. Disabled people who have a recognised trade certificate can show potential employers that they are up to the demands of the job. Certification, however, is not often appropriate for those who aim to become self-employed. They need to learn how to make use of the simple materials and equipment that they are likely to be able to afford and how to survive in the competitive conditions of the market-place, where customers want value for money rather than paper qualifications.

Disabled people will presumably need more rather than less training than the able-bodied, partly because of their physical disabilities and partly because of the need for emotional rehabilitation, which has already been referred to. It is unlikely, however, that many institutions interested in preparing disabled people for self-employment would serve their clients better by extending the training period since it is very difficult for institutionalised training to be wholly relevant to self-employment. In addition, the trainees would probably become more dependent on the institution and thus less able to cope on their own. The longer someone spends in an institution, the longer it takes for him or her to "re-enter" the real world, and this is another reason for making vocational training for the disabled as brief as possible, consistent with attaining the necessary level of skill and self-confidence.

Capital

We have already seen in the previous chapter that the disabled self-employed themselves see shortage of capital as their major problem. There is a great deal of evidence that many small-scale business people are wrong when they claim that if only they had more capital all their problems would be solved. Closer analysis of their enterprises shows that they are not making the optimum use of whatever capital they do have and that they would similarly fail to make good use of more capital; what they need is better ability to manage finance, not more finance.

We have no definitive information about the ways in which our sample of disabled business people were using their capital, but most of them are operating on a very small scale. The few figures we have, as well as visual indications, suggest that they are not in fact misusing their existing capital by having too many of the wrong materials in stock or by extending excessive credit to slow-paying customers.

Because disabled people tend to be poorer than others and to have had less opportunity for accumulating any capital of their own, the problem of scarce capital is likely to be more serious for them. One of the most important things a support institution can provide, therefore, is money or access to it. The following figures show how the 32 institutions are helping their clients to deal with this problem:

- provide money grants   3
- provide grants in kind   6
- provide grants of money and in kind   3
- provide loans   5
- assist trainees to obtain bank loans   3
- no financial assistance   12

It is important to remember that the great majority of the clients of most of these institutions do not become self-employed; the financial assistance is therefore confined to the small minority who do, except for tool-kits which are often given to jobseekers, and it is not surprising that over a third of the institutions do not provide financial assistance at all.

As a general rule, grants are increasingly becoming discredited as an effective means of helping people to become self-employed; many voluntary agencies and government organisations are attempting, with great difficulty, to change from grants to loans because they have been persuaded of the advantages of credit as opposed to gifts.

The disadvantages of grants are many and well known; fewer people can benefit because the funds are not repaid for re-lending, and because there is no need to repay the grant the recipients tend not to take their proposed enterprises seriously and may divert the funds to expenditure which will not generate income.

Even loans at low rates of interest are now seen to be of questionable value; although the lower rate of interest is of some benefit to the borrower, the disadvantages to the lender, and thus to other potential borrowers, far outweigh the short-term benefits to the few who can borrow. The lending institution earns little or no income from the transaction, certainly not enough to cover the costs involved, and there is thus no incentive for commercial banks or others to support or take over the operation. The borrowers are under no pressure to repay because there is no mounting burden of unpaid interest, and they are ill prepared to move from the specialised "sheltered" lending institution into the real world of commercial interest rates.

The types of enterprise which poor people start are also very labour-intensive in that they tend to require very little capital in relation to the earnings generated from employment. If such an enterprise is moderately successful, repaying a loan – even when interest payments are added to the repayment of the principal – is likely to make little difference to the owner's income.

Several of the foregoing case studies illustrate this point. Fely Lucas from the Philippines, for instance, earns a monthly profit of P800 from her business which she started with a loan of P500. The "return on investment" for this business is about 2,000 per cent, which is of course absurdly high by normal economic standards because it includes payment for the owner's own time. Nevertheless, it would have been very easy for Fely Lucas to repay the loan of P500 she received for the initial capital within a few months with little impact on her earnings.

Loans, and even quite high rates of interest, can usually be repaid with little difficulty so long as the enterprise succeeds. If it fails, however, payments which would have been insignificant in relation even to very modest earnings may become quite impossible since they will have to be made out of whatever meagre income the borrower was subsisting on before trying to start the business. A number of the disabled entrepreneurs described in the case studies have dependants as well as themselves to support so that enforced repayment would have a serious impact on them as well as on the disabled person.

However, many if not most of the people described in the case studies failed at their first attempt at self-employment and some, like Luwo Jambo, the shoemaker, failed many times before finally finding a business and a location where it could survive. It would have been quite impossible for any of the people who failed at the first attempt to repay a loan at that time, or even for many years thereafter. It might be argued that the lending institution should use discretion when deciding whom to press for repayment and whose debts to cancel, but experience shows that the whole concept of credit can easily be destroyed beyond repair if the lender is continually forced to write off the debts of those who fail to repay when their failure is not their own fault. It is far better to make grants openly and from the start than to start a loan programme which becomes a hybrid system of loans and grants, with inevitable ill-will between those whose debts are written off and those who have to repay.

The failure rate for businesses, with resulting inability to repay, is likely to be higher for disabled people than for the able-bodied, all things being equal and in spite of their undoubtedly enhanced persistence and commitment. It may therefore be appropriate for financial assistance for those starting their own enterprises, at least for the first time, to be offered in the form of grants. Many professional investors in new enterprise favour entrepreneurs who have failed before because of the valuable lessons they have learned; if a disabled person fails, this should not disqualify him or her from receiving a further grant, or possibly a loan, because the chances of success the second time are so much enhanced.

Nine of the 12 institutions which make grants give at least a part in kind, in the form of equipment or initial supplies of materials. This may seem to imply that the recipients cannot be trusted to spend the money as they should, but people who are close to destitution may well be tempted to act against their own long-term interests. If someone is given the tools to start a carpentry business, or a sewing-machine to start tailoring, he or she is far more likely actually to start than if a money grant were given and the recipient had to find a supplier and then identify and purchase the correct equipment without any help.

Essential supplies are also very often in short supply and one of the major roles of a support institution may be to provide privileged access to scarce items. Such scarcities are usually the result of misplaced government policies, but if supply is a problem, disabled people are the least likely group to obtain their due share of whatever is available. It may be, therefore, that grants of equipment – possibly supplemented by a small loan for working capital to buy raw materials or goods to be resold – is the most appropriate form of financial assistance for many disabled people.

Marketing

We saw in the last chapter that the shortage of customers was the second most important problem for the 53 self-employed people who were surveyed. The 32 institutions were asked what forms of assistance they provided in addition to skills training and finance, and the following figures very briefly summarise the number which are offering, in one way or another, services in the specified areas:

- Management assistance   26
- Marketing assistance   17
- Assistance with licences   17
- Assistance with premises   15
- Management training   12
- Assistance with raw materials   11

It might be argued that management training and the regular counselling through which management assistance is normally provided should enable clients to solve their own marketing problems, but most management training and assistance focus on bookkeeping and records rather than on marketing, and there does seem to be a marked discrepancy between the disabled entrepreneurs' own perceptions of their problems and the services provided. Finance is the most important problem and the most frequently provided service, but after that the emphasis seems to be rather on what the institutions can provide than on what the business people say they need.

This is not particularly surprising since marketing and selling are the most difficult and, at the same time, the most important tasks for any business and perhaps those with which a typical social worker or trainer is least qualified to assist. Only two or three institutions claimed to be doing more than providing introductions to customers, but since it is such a pressing problem, there may be some other things that can be done.

Many people are unaware of the potential impact of their own institution's purchasing power; it is all too common for an organisation to spend large sums of money, and still more administrative time on providing for itself services such as a canteen, a messenger service, transport, cleaning or stationery which could be cheaply and more efficiently provided by local entrepreneurs. The management of any organisation which diverts its energy from its main task in order to provide services that could better be provided by outsiders is to be blamed, but it is all the more paradoxical when the management of institutions whose task is to develop local entrepreneurs falls into the same error.

Every rehabilitation institution should therefore carefully examine its own purchases, not neglecting the humblest goods and services such as brushes or cleaning, and should ensure that as much of its purchasing power as possible is used for the benefit of its own ex-trainees, whether they are running their own enterprises or working for others.

The above list showed that as many institutions are assisting with licences and other government formalities as with marketing; if institutions have any influence with government agencies, they ought to be able to persuade them to divert some of their local purchases to enterprises run by disabled people. Here again, it might appear that the simple goods and services provided by the disabled cannot be of any use to a government department, but if somebody takes the time to list all the goods and services which can be bought from disabled people and those which are bought by any institution there will almost always be some items on both lists. Even if these purchases involve slightly more administrative effort, or are at marginally higher prices or lower quality, the difference in cost will be less than the cost of supporting the disabled workers through direct subsidies.

"Marketing" may be too complex a term to apply to much of what has to be done in the type of small enterprise which disabled people are likely to start when leaving a rehabilitation institution. So long as there is a demand for the product, the main determinant of success will be the entrepreneur's ability to sell it. Selling requires confidence, and confidence is what many disabled people lack; this makes it all the more important that institutions should concentrate on building or rebuilding the self-confidence of their clients so that they will be able to start on their own and to sell whatever they produce.

There are a number of by now well-proven training techniques whereby the personal characteristics which are needed for success in self-employment, such as persistence, commitment to quality, awareness of opportunities and self-confidence, can be created, enhanced or at least revealed. These techniques have been used with some success with tribal groups and others who are for some reason excluded from the mainstream of economic activity in certain countries. None of the rehabilitation institutions covered in our survey was apparently using these techniques of behavioural training, but they can be a valuable supplement to the kind of personal confidence building that clearly plays so large a part in the eventual success of disabled business people such as Babu Suryawanshi, whose emotional trauma is often as serious as their physical disability.

Follow-up

Once a person has acquired the necessary skills and has been assisted to obtain whatever equipment and material are needed, it may be possible for him or her to become self-employed and for the enterprise to survive. It might be argued, in fact, that those who have been fortunate enough to receive institutional assistance of this kind have no right to expect any further support; whatever resources are available should be used to give other people the same opportunity.

In fact, however, it is very difficult for most people to move from the shelter and support of an institution to total independence. Employed people can to an extent depend upon their colleagues and the employer for some support, but the self-employed have nobody with whom to share their difficulties; they must be economically and emotionally independent. People like Bob Sabio, the figurine maker, and Lamin Sambou, the tailor, never had the benefit of assistance from an institution and therefore never had the problem of "re-entry" into the harsh reality of the world outside after a period of relative shelter.

Those who have been institutionalised, however, often need a "bridge" between the institution and the real world, particularly when it is the lonely world of self-employment. Some form of post-training support is therefore usually desirable. Twenty of the 32 institutions provided some follow-up of this kind, usually by regular visits from an adviser or counsellor. Such visits may be necessary to carry out medical checks, to collect loan repayments, to pay out pensions or other subventions or for some other administrative purposes, but they often have the far more important effect of maintaining a friendly link and providing a sympathetic ear.

It is also important for the staff of any institution to maintain contact with its ex-trainees. We saw earlier that around one-third of the institutions covered in our survey were unable to state how many or what proportion of their trainees finally became self-employed; it is obviously difficult to keep in touch with every trainee who leaves an institution and it would have been quite impossible for any institution to keep in touch with Luwo Jambo in his many travels from his birthplace in Mozambique, or with Lamin Sambou in his moves from Senegal to the Gambia and back.

Nevertheless, it is impossible to evaluate and adapt rehabilitation and training programmes without regular and frequent contact with people who have been trained and the world in which they have to make their way. Follow-up visits to ex-trainees serve the dual purpose of bridging the gap for both groups of people, the trainees and the trainers.

It is also important not to continue support indefinitely, both to avoid perpetuating dependence and to ensure that resources are not unfairly wasted on a small number of people. Twenty-four of the institutions in our survey claimed that they had a definite policy of terminating post-training support after a certain period which might vary according to the nature and the problems of the client. It may be significant that none of the entrepreneurs described in the case studies mentioned post-training support of this kind, except for Momodou Njie, who relied on the adviser from the IBAS to help him with his accounts. It may be that regular contact is necessary not so much for particular services or advice but just for the caring and contact which allow the new entrepreneur gradually to become accustomed to the solitary world of self-employment.

6

Lessons to be learned

We hope that most readers will have picked up a number of points from the foregoing pages which will help them to plan and implement more effective programmes of assistance for disabled people who wish to become, or already are, self-employed. In this chapter, however, we should like to stress again a number of issues which have been mentioned, because they seem to be of particular importance and because some of them are based on what has been learned over many years of experience in assisting new and smaller enterprises. Annex I consists of brief guide-lines for all those called upon to assist disabled people in setting up a business.

Self-employment is not for everyone

First of all, at the risk of over-stressing the obvious, we must yet again emphasise that self-employment is not for everybody, whether he or she is disabled or not. Most of the case studies describe people who have achieved remarkable success against heavy odds; they are and should be admired because of this, but it is vital to avoid the impression that entrepreneurs are in some way "better" than other people. It is unlikely that more than a very few of the readers of this book will be entrepreneurs; most will be social workers, trainers or others employed in helping the disabled to become self-sufficient.

This does not mean that such people are in any way less useful or less praiseworthy than someone who starts and sustains his or her own enterprise, and clients of rehabilitation institutions must not be given the impression that they should in any way feel obligated to emulate the self-employed or feel inadequate because they do not. Everyone must decide what he or she wants to do, and the role of the counsellor or trainer is not to compel or even to persuade but to present alternatives and develop clients' capacity to choose for themselves.

The purpose of this book, therefore, has not been to "promote" the idea of self-employment for the disabled. Instead, it gives some examples of what can be done so that disabled people themselves, their families and those who wish to assist them may be aware of the opportunities and the difficulties in order to widen the selection of ways in which disabled people can work towards self-sufficiency.

The disabled are not very different from other people

Although this book is about the disabled self-employed, many of the case studies and the data from the larger sample might equally well have been drawn from a sample of enterprises owned by the non-disabled in the same countries. There are certain advantages and disadvantages which may make self-employment more or less attractive to disabled than to non-disabled people, but a similar list could be put together for any group of people; the similarities are far more striking than the differences.

Most disabled people who are in business for themselves, like most other entrepreneurs, never received help from official institutions but merely made the best of their resources, using whatever family or other support was available. Those who work for official institutions should regularly remind themselves of this fact and should retain a due sense of humility about what they can do. Above all, they should avoid the temptation to refer to and think of the businesses started by their own clients as "their" businesses; the businesses belong to their owners, who took the risks and deserve the credit. The outsider's contribution can never be more than a modest one, and the best assistance agency is one whose clients deny that it ever helped them.

The types of enterprise started by the disabled are as numerous and varied as those started by anyone else, and their problems seem to be very similar to those of other enterprises. Ill-health seems to be relatively unusual as a problem, perhaps because disabled people take care to select enterprises which they can cope with, and the main difficulties of finance and marketing are exactly those which affect all small enterprises everywhere.

Vending and petty trade are particularly common forms of self-employment for the disabled, as for other people, and tend also to be neglected or even despised by outsiders; it is very encouraging, and in fact unusual, to find a number of institutions preparing trainees specifically for vending and to read lists of successful enterprises run by ex-trainees which include so many varieties of trading as opposed to manufacturing activities.

The case studies also illustrate another common feature of new enterprises everywhere regardless of who starts them, namely that a high rate of failure can be expected. Persistence is one of the main determinants of entrepreneurial success and this, as often as not, has to be demonstrated through unwillingness to give up in spite of repeated failure; others may regard such behaviour as stubborn rather than intelligent, but people who wish to assist the self-employed must be ready to face a high rate of failure among their clients and to recognise that the person who tries again and again will probably succeed one day.

Institutions should be local and flexible

Many of the rehabilitation institutions in our sample appear to be small and to operate on a local level. Those that are larger usually have numbers of relatively independent branches, whether they be run by government or by voluntary agencies, and this means that they are close to the people they are trying to help.

The general experience of small enterprise assistance agencies, particularly those working with the poorer members of society, is that you have to be small and poor to help poor people to start small enterprises. Voluntary agencies are generally poorer and always smaller than governments, and the few very critical reports from the interviewers related mainly to government institutions which were unable to adapt flexibly to the needs of their clients. Voluntary organisations seem in general to be more effective at this type of work than governments.

There are many advantages in a diversity of funding sources, including earnings from the sale of goods or services produced by trainees in the course of their rehabilitation. Scarcity of resources, together with concern for tangible results rather than mere institutional survival, means that the most effective rehabilitation training is as brief as possible and is related to the needs of the market and the wishes of the trainees rather than to the facilities and skills of the institution.

We have already referred to the tremendous diversity of types of enterprise; the types of training should reflect this diversity rather than attempting to force trainees into an inappropriate but institutionally convenient mould, and this probably means that the institution itself will have the facilities and the staff to train only a small proportion of its trainees. The remainder will have to be trained in an ad hoc manner; none of the institutions in our survey mentioned the use of existing enterprises as places for training, but experience shows that established business people are usually very happy to allow others to train with them, as in traditional apprenticeship schemes, through which many of the disabled entrepreneurs in our case studies received their training.

Some business people may accept trainees for nothing, out of good will and as a source of free labour; others may demand a small fee, while still others may be willing to pay a nominal wage. In any case, if the training businesses are properly selected and supervised, the training is likely to be more relevant and less expensive than can be provided within an institution. Large numbers of co-operating training businesses may not be as impressive as neat and well-equipped workshops, but they are probably far more effective.

Finance may be granted but loans must be repaid

It would be inappropriate to generalise on the basis of so little evidence, and every institution and indeed every prospective self-employed disabled man or woman is different and requires a different "package" of assistance. There does appear, however, to be a good case for making grants rather than loans, at least for people who are starting an enterprise for the first time. These grants should be modest and should preferably be in kind rather than in cash.

Loans are more appropriate for those who need money for expansion or to enter a new business in addition to an already established one, as so many of the people in our case studies wish to do. It is vital that a loan programme should be a serious and rigourously managed enterprise in its own right with commercial rates of interest. Prospective borrowers should be helped if necessary to appraise their proposals carefully, but they should be made to realise that they will have to repay, whatever may happen, and that the lending institution will have to take steps to recover its money if repayments are not made in time.

Social pressure may be a more effective incentive to repay than threats from the lender, particularly if it comes from fellow members of a revolving loan scheme who demand repayments so that they can in their turn benefit from a loan. No mention was made of this type of scheme, perhaps because many if not most disabled people are relatively isolated from one another, but it might be appropriate to try to implement such a scheme as a source of working capital and expansion finance for a trial group of disabled self-employed people, perhaps building on any informal associations of ex-trainees of a rehabilitation institution that are working in the same area.

The prospective able-bodied self-employed are usually selected partly at least on the basis of their emotional suitability, which includes self-confidence. Disabled people often suffer from a lack of self-confidence that may be even more debilitating than the disability itself. This may be the most critical difference between the assistance needs of the disabled and of other people, and it calls for close personal contact and sensitive encouragement without denying clients the opportunity to choose for themselves.

This may also call for greater use of behavioural training techniques such as achievement motivation and entrepreneurship development training, but these can never be a substitute for the individual contact and support which clearly played a major part in the success of many of the business people described in the case studies.

Assistance must "bridge the gap"

Disabled people lack self-confidence and most of them lack mobility; able-bodied people, particularly those who are in positions of responsibility, often feel an obligation to help the disabled and welcome opportunities to do so which are effective but involve a minimum of trouble and expense.

This means that one of the most effective ways in which an assistance agency can help is by bridging the gap between the disabled person and the large number of institutions that have the necessary resources. It is far better for a rehabilitation institution to use its good offices to help its trainees obtain bank loans than for it to try to become a banker itself, and it makes more sense to persuade the authorities responsible for allocating industrial sheds to give space to disabled business people than for the rehabilitation institution to set up its own industrial estate.

Similar help can be and is being provided with licences, raw materials and many other services, including introductions to customers, but marketing, as is so often the case, appears to be the most neglected area. Much is being done, particularly through contacts and introductions, but more can be done by mobilising the institution's own purchasing power and by persuading governments and other large buyers to purchase from the disabled. If a business has a market, it can usually raise finance, find a location, acquire skills and obtain raw materials and equipment, but without any sales all these things are in vain. Those wanting to help the self-employed must ensure that their clients recognise the fundamental importance of marketing.

They must also adopt a "marketing orientation" themselves, in relation to their clients, who are the "customers" of a rehabilitation institution even if they do not pay.

Marketing often means reaching out to customers rather than waiting for them to beat a pathway to your door. A rehabilitation institution must reach out to its customers by following up trainees, visiting them in their places of work and trying to provide relevant and practical assistance whenever possible. Staff with a marketing outlook on their job will not only help their clients to market their goods and services to their customers, but will also market the institution's services more effectively to its clients, to government and to donors. Thus a greater volume of more efficient assistance will be made available to help more disabled people become profitably self-employed, and thus to achieve both economic and personal independence.

7

Some thoughts for planners

The global scene

The number of people around the world who are physically or mentally disabled has surpassed the 500 million mark. It increases every year by some 15 million – victims of wars, accidents, malnutrition and disease.

Disabled people in developing countries usually lack a common voice with which to put their case to society. Unless they join associations – and many now do – they have no platform from which to defend themselves. It is therefore hardly surprising that their legitimate claims are treated as an afterthought by politicians and planners, obsessed by budget deficits, debt repayments and massive unemployment – the grim legacy of the recession and its aftermath.

Few Third World communities can afford fully to maintain the one in ten of their members who are likely to be disabled. Some of them must be fed, clothed and given special care. All this imposes a heavy burden on families and public services. The traditional back-up systems of kinship solidarity are being strained to breaking-point.

In human terms the problem is one of suffering and misery. The feelings of inadequacy, dependency and insecurity that many disabled persons experience often compel them to shun society or turn to begging as a means of livelihood.

In developing countries facilities for the disabled are woefully inadequate or non-existent. The vast majority of disabled people are bypassed by what little relief is available.

Yet governments are increasingly compelled to introduce austerity measures, often at the expense of social programmes. In times of economic recession some planners are tempted to abandon social development and to await better times for its reinstatement. However, economic strength and social development are inseparable. Any effort, however small, to create fair social conditions for the population will benefit economic recovery. It is not true that economically weak countries cannot afford the luxury of social programmes; what they cannot afford is luxury social programmes. Thus, economic crisis, as much as it creates harm and misery, may force planners to rethink social expenditures and may expose them to the challenge of doing more with less money.

Many governments are still trapped by the conventional thinking that to provide welfare benefits to the "unfortunate" is proof of their will and ability to practise humanitarian ideals. But for the handicapped millions neither welfare nor charity is the answer, for these measures tend to perpetuate rather than reduce dependency.

Such resources could be used more effectively if they were channelled to programmes which support self-help and self-reliance of the disabled. Since current costs of institutional care and rehabilitation are becoming prohibitive, there should be a move towards community-based services. Another cost-effective course of action is integration of the disabled into conventional schools and training programmes. There is also scope for stimulating involvement of private firms in vocational rehabilitation and the development of basic skills.

The need for innovative, realistic approaches is urgent. The number of handicapped people seeking help could swell to some 700 million by the turn of the century.

Self-reliance versus dependence

Unclear and unfeasible social objectives will inevitably lead to wrong investments and eventually do more harm than good.

Such unclear objectives are to be suspected when services for disabled persons are thought to be exclusively the responsibility of social welfare ministries or departments, the expectation being that disabled people, like the aged, the sick, the destitute and the delinquents, are people with problems requiring the assistance of a social worker. Social workers may indeed have an important role to play at a specific moment of the rehabilitation process, but – as the case studies and the arguments advanced in this book have shown – a disabled person striving to achieve self-reliance needs other types of assistance.

In fact, the rehabilitation concept has a different objective from the social work concept, the one providing assistance towards independence, the other assistance to a dependant.

This book shows that self-reliance through self-employment is a feasible proposition for many disabled people. It also demonstrates that the assistance such an approach requires is minimal compared to costly institutional and long-term support programmes.

Planners should recognise that the objective of self-reliance for disabled people has important political implications: it combines a social and humanitarian goal with that of economic development. The assistance needed by the disabled who wish to engage in income-generating activities is an economic investment, not social welfare.

Unfortunately, the present structures are extremely inadequate for providing the type of services disabled people actually require, and this is why planners are called upon to examine how a more cost-effective and at the same time more efficient system can be established.

Social welfare departments may not want to lose their responsibility for disability matters, nor may traditional non-governmental organisations and private institutions be prepared to change their established patterns of service delivery, which are often based on benevolent motives. Yet unless a really innovative effort is made

– and this book has plenty of suggestions in this respect – the objective of self-reliance cannot be seriously pursued, a situation which neither the economies of developing countries nor the disabled themselves can afford.

Of course, it is not suggested that self-reliance is a feasible goal for all disabled people. Some may at best achieve partial economic independence, while others may be able to make only a very small contribution to earning their living and some may make none at all; consequently, it is entirely legitimate to continue to provide welfare services for those disabled people who will always be in need of this type of support.

The large majority of disabled people, however, have the ability and the desire to earn a living, to have a family and therefore not only to support themselves but also their partners and children. It is for these that present disability programmes are inadequate.

Rethinking planning priorities

This book may have some important implications for those concerned with planning rehabilitation services in developing countries – be they ministry officials, staff and advisers from international governmental or non-governmental organisations, or staff of donor agencies. It opens a new spectrum of possibilities for establishing practical and appropriate services designed to promote self-help and economic self-reliance for disabled people.

Whether these services should be developed outside the traditional rehabilitation agencies and programmes, or from within, depends very much on the latter's flexibility and readiness to adjust and reorient their work. In any case, new ways will have to be explored of co-operating with those other existing institutions and facilities which are concerned with assisting the able bodied to become self-employed.

Rehabilitation centres can learn from this book that they can achieve better results for their disabled clients if they cease to provide services after an appropriate level of confidence building and training and other necessary rehabilitation goals have been achieved; thereafter they can act as agents and go-betweens on behalf of their clients to ensure that they have access to ordinary community resources. This will mean that such centres will have to reorient their programme to provide more extension and follow-up services than they do now. They should employ staff familiar with the world of work and business, or at least ensure that their staff are aware of the reality of life; their rehabilitation programmes should be geared to preparing their disabled clients to face the world outside.

At the same time a far greater effort is required to reach out into communities with the objective of finding the most appropriate way to economic independence for each individual disabled person who is capable of it and then of helping him or her to achieve it.

The challenge for planners is therefore how to reorganise services for disabled people of working age so as to respond more adequately to their real employment needs. Disabled people must be given an equal opportunity for training and employment and access to training facilities, enterprise-based training, and grants and loans for self-employment. Non-institutional, community-oriented rehabilitation programmes must be organised, and skills training must be more appropriate. Last but not least, the findings of this book must be translated into concrete projects and programmes to achieve a visible increase in the numbers of disabled people engaged in self-employment or other income-generating schemes.

Guide-lines for assistance to self-development

Selection

- Self-employment is not for all, or even the majority, of the disabled.

- Self-selection is the best form of selection; it is necessary to ensure that those who ask for assistance are actually capable of becoming self-employed by asking them to do the preparatory work, gather information and so on, as far as is practical, so that they realise for themselves what is involved and drop out if they cannot manage.

- People who have no idea about what sort of business they might undertake are unlikely to be able to make a success of any business.

- Experience and commitment are far more important than education and qualifications.

- Earlier failure is the best preparation for future success.

- Persistence and initiative are the most important qualities, and these can be appraised from anyone's past history.

The choice of business

- The best idea is the one someone has himself or herself; the business that seems the most promising to an outsider will be no good if the potential entrepreneur does not believe in it.

- The market is the most important factor in any enterprise, however small; without customers, no business can even start.

- Every business must have a "unique selling point": Why will people buy its products or services, rather than someone else's? If there is no reason, there will probably be no customers either.

- Market research is often too vague; the prospective self-employed should know who, specifically and by name, will be his or her customers.

Capital

- Money should only be lent if it can reasonably be expected to be repaid; otherwise, grants are better.

■ Every enterprise needs fixed capital for equipment, and working capital to keep it going during the time between payment for supplies and receipts from customers. Working capital is often the more important of the two, and is often neglected.

■ Loan repayments should be calculated so that the borrower is better off than before the business started, even after making the repayments.

■ Those who become self-employed should invest something of their own, even if it is only initial unpaid work; if the business costs an individual nothing, he or she will not fight to keep it alive.

■ Loans should be quick to obtain and easy to repay; slow procedures and bureaucracy are far more serious than high interest rates, as the continuing success of moneylenders shows.

Training

■ People must learn what they can use, not what the institution is equipped to teach.

■ Existing businesses are often better training-grounds than any special training workshop.

■ Business records are only of value if the self-employed can use them as well as keep them. If they cannot, it is a waste of time to prepare them.

■ People cannot be taught; they must learn for themselves.

■ Self-confidence is more important than specific skills; if people believe they can do something, they usually can.

Follow-up

■ Entrepreneurs must be allowed to fail; "give it up" is often the best advice.

■ People need continuing contact with others who are self-employed; this is often more helpful than advice from an outsider.

■ It is important for the self-employed, and for assistance agencies, to recognise when assistance is no longer necessary, and to stop it.

■ The self-employed need to be asked to talk about their problems, not told what to do.

■ There are many institutions which help the self-employed; introductions to the specialists are better than help from the ignorant.

Institutions surveyed

Jairos Jiri Association, Harare, Zimbabwe.

The Indigenous Business Advisory Service, The Gambia.

The Salvation Army, Thika, Kenya.

Variety Village, Thika, Kenya.

Machakos Trade Training Centre, Kenya.

Embu Rural Vocational Rehabilitation Centre, Kenya.

Murirandas Rehabilitation Centre, Muranga, Kenya.

Kericho Rural Vocational Rehabilitation Centre, Kenya.

Kakamega Rural Vocational Rehabilitation Centre, Kenya.

The Industrial Rehabilitation Centre, Nairobi, Kenya.

Kisii Rural Vocational Rehabilitation Centre, Kenya. Likoni Quality Furniture, Kenya.

Ministry of Social Services and Development, Region XII, Philippines.

Soroptimist International of Bacolod City, Philippines.

Ephpheta Incorporated, Philippines.

Negros Occidental Rehabilitation Foundation, Philippines.

Worth Trust, Katpadi, India.

Social Service Centre, Madras, India.

Sacred Heart Leprosy Centre, Sakkottai, Tamil Nadu, India.

St. Louis Institute for the Deaf and the Blind, Madras, India.

Bishop Diehl Rehabilitation Home for the Blind, Tiruchirapalli, Tamil Nadu, India.

Annai J.K.K. Samporami Ammal Charitable Trust, Komarapalayam, Tamil Nadu, India.

Vocational Rehabilitation Centre for the Handicapped, Bombay, India.

National Society for Equal Opportunities for the Handicapped, Bombay, India.

Society for the Vocational Rehabilitation of the Handicapped, Bombay, India.

The NSD Industrial Home for the Blind, Bombay, India.

The Indian Cancer Society Rehabilitation Centre, Bombay, India.

The Fellowship of the Physically Handicapped, Bombay, India.

Apang Maitri, Bombay, India.

Bombay Leprosy Project, India.

The All India Institute of Physical Medicine and Rehabilitation, Bombay.

The National Association for the Blind, Bombay, India.

Further reading

Dembetzer, B.: *Marketing handicraft from developing countries: A handbook for producers* (London, Intermediate Technology (IT) Publications, 1983).

Devereux, S.; Pares, H.; Best, J.: *Manual of credit and savings for the poor of developing countries* (Oxford, Oxfam, 1987).

Harper, M.: *Consultancy for small business* (London, IT Publications, 1976).

idem: *Entrepreneurship for the poor* (London, IT Publications, 1984).

idem: *Small business in the Third World: Guide-lines for practical assistance* (Chichester, Wiley, 1984).

Technonet Asia/University of the Philippines, Institute for Small-Scale Industries: *Entrepreneur's handbook* (Singapore, 1981).

(All these books can be obtained from IT Publications, 103-105 Southampton Row, London WC1B 4HH, United Kingdom).

D.E.N. Dickson (ed.): *Improve your business,* Handbook and Workbook (Geneva, ILO, 1986).

ILO: *Creating a market,* A programmed book, (Geneva, 1968).

idem: *The promotion of small and medium-sized enterprises,* Report VI, International Labour Conference, 72nd Session, Geneva, 1986.

ILO/MATCOM manuals and self-study material on co-operative management, in particular, the manuals on workers' co-operatives which provide guide-lines for trainers in this field.

Kenneth Loucks: *Training entrepreneurs for small business creation: Lessons from experience,* Management Development Series No. 26 (Geneva, ILO, 1988).

Geoffrey Meredith et al.: *The practice of entrepreneurship* (Geneva, ILO, 1982).

Philip Neck and Robert Nelson (eds.): *Small enterprise development: Policies and programmes,* Management Development Series No. 14 (Geneva, ILO, second (revised) ed., 1987).

(All these books can be obtained from ILO Publications, International Labour Office, CH-1211 Geneva 22, Switzerland.)